The Story of the World

TEST BOOK AND ANSWER KEY

Volume 4: The Modern Age

D1567242

WELL-TRAINED MIND PRESS

Charles City, Virginia
www.welltrainedmind.com

How to Use These Tests and Answer Key

These Tests and their accompanying Answer Key are designed to go along with Volume 4 of Susan Wise Bauer's *The Story of the World: History for the Classical Child*. These tests are designed for those teachers and parents who want to evaluate their students' understanding of the major ideas and dates found within the *Story of the World* text. After your student reads each chapter of the book, he should be given time to review the reading before taking that chapter's test. If you are using the *Story of the World Volume 4 Activity Book*, you should go through the chapter's Review Questions, Complete the Outline exercises, Map Activities, Timeline, and other complementary projects and readings. These will reinforce and expand your child's knowledge of the material. For more information on the *Volume 4 Activity Book* (ISBN 978-0-9728603-5-2), please visit www.welltrainedmind.com. We recommend reading one chapter of the text each week and taking the appropriate test at the end of the week.

Photocopying and Distribution Policy

The Story of the World

Chapter 1 Test: Britain's Empire

A. **Sequencing. Number the events in the correct order using 1 for the event that happened first, 6 for the event that happened last, and so on.**

_____ Indian soldiers rebelled against the East India Company and took control of Delhi.

_____ English merchants joined together into a group called the East India Company and built trading posts along the Indian coast.

_____ The British government removed the emperor of India and made India a British colony.

_____ The governor of Bengal assembled an army and tried to force the English to leave Calcutta.

_____ The East India Company began using a new kind of rifle known as the Enfield rifle.

_____ The East India Company took control of the government of Bengal.

B. **Fill in the blanks.**

7. The _____ was built to house all of the exhibits at the Great Exhibition of the Works of Industry of All Nations.

8. This building was unusual because it was made of _____.

9. _____ was the queen of Great Britain during the Great Exhibition.

10. The native Indian soldiers who worked for the East India Company were known as _____.

11. _____ was the last emperor of India.

12. After the British took control of India, the _____ of India became the head official who helped the Queen and Parliament rule India.

C. **Short Answer. Answer each question using a complete sentence.**

13. Why were the people of London worried about the special building that housed the exhibits at the Great Exhibition?

_____

_____

_____

14. What was the real reason for the Great Exhibition?

_____

_____

_____

15. Where did Great Britain have colonies? Name at least four places.

_____

_____

_____

16. Why did Indian soldiers not want to serve on British ships?

_____

_____

_____

17. What happened to the last emperor of India?

_____

_____

_____

D. Essay. Answer the following question in paragraph form.

18. Why did the Enfield rifle cause such a problem in India?

_____

_____

_____

_____

_____

The Story of the World

Chapter 2 Test: West Against East

A. **Sequencing. Number the events in the correct order using 1 for the event that happened first, 6 for the event that happened last, and so on.**

_____ Russian and French Christians argued about who should protect the Church of the Nativity in Bethlehem.

_____ The British and the French joined together to push back the Russians.

_____ The ruler of Turkey gave several Christian countries permission to take care of different holy places in Palestine.

_____ Hundreds of British soldiers were killed at the Battle of Balaklava.

_____ The Russian army invaded the northern part of the Turkish Empire.

_____ Alexander, the czar's son, fired the chief general of the Russian army because he made so many horrible mistakes.

B. **Fill in the blanks.**

7. The _____ family ruled Japan for over 200 years.

8. In 1853, Commodore _____ sailed into Edo Bay with four huge warships.

9. He had been sent to Japan by President _____ of the United States.

10. The Commodore was finally taken to see _____, the governor of a nearby Japanese town.

11. When the Crimean War began, _____ was the czar of Russia.

12. The French and British hoped to capture the Russian city of _____.

13. A peace treaty called the _____ ended the Crimean War.

C. **Short Answer. Answer each question using a complete sentence.**

14. In the mid-nineteenth century, who had all of the power in Japan?

_____

_____

_____

15. Why did Japanese rulers want to keep Westerners out of Japan?

_____

_____

_____

16. What did American merchants want to buy from Japan?

_____

_____

_____

17. Why did the Russians want to capture Constantinople?

_____

_____

_____

18. After fighting with each other for hundreds of years, why did the French and the English suddenly become friends?

_____

_____

_____

D. Essay. Answer the following question in paragraph form.

19. When the Crimean War began, why were the countries so ready to fight with each other? (Give four reasons in your answer.)

_____

_____

_____

_____

_____

Name _____   Date _____

The Story of the World

Chapter 3 Test: British Invasions

A. **Sequencing. Number the events in the correct order using 1 for the event that happened first, 6 for the event that happened last, and so on.**

_____ A native Afghan known as Durrani ruled over the different tribes of Afghanistan for twenty-six years.

_____ The British offered to loan money to Dost Mohammad so that he could fight against his enemies.

_____ The leaders of Afghanistan agreed to recognize Dost Mohammad as their leader and gave him the title Amir.

_____ A heroic Afghan chief named Mirwais Khan drove the Persians out of Afghanistan.

_____ The Indian-British army marched into Afghanistan.

_____ The Russian government persuaded Persia to join Russia in an invasion of western Afghanistan.

B. **Fill in the blanks.**

7. _____ was the largest and most important city in Afghanistan.

8. The Russian and British strategies to get control of Afghanistan became known as the _____.

9. David Livingstone was a missionary from _____.

10. Livingstone wrote a book about his travels in Africa called _____.

11. _____ was an American journalist who went to Africa in search of Livingstone.

12. He finally found Livingstone at Ujiji, a village just east of the _____ River.

C. **Short Answer. Answer each question using a complete sentence.**

13. Why were Russia and Great Britain so interested in Afghanistan?

_____

_____

_____

14. When the British offered to loan money to Dost Mohammad, what did he do?

_____

_____

_____

15. Why was the British army so unpopular in Afghanistan?

_____

_____

_____

16. What was David Livingstone's official job when he was made a consul by the British government?

_____

_____

_____

17. Why did the *New York Times* send one of its journalists to look for Livingstone?

_____

_____

_____

D. Essay. Answer the following question in paragraph form.

18. How did David Livingstone hope to end the slave trade?

_____

_____

_____

_____

_____

Name _____   Date _____

The Story of the World

Chapter 4 Test: Resurrection and Rebellion

A.   **Sequencing. Number the events in the correct order using 1 for the event that happened first, 6 for the event that happened last, and so on.**

____ The Carbonaria joined all of the secret societies together in a revolt against Austria.

____ After receiving a message from the pope, the king of France sent soldiers to Rome.

____ Italians who wanted to break free of Austria began to meet together in secret societies.

____ Hundreds of Sicilians joined the Italian army to fight against the Austrians.

____ The Italians defeated the Austrians at the Battle of Volturno.

____ The Austrian army used balloons to drop bombs on the revolutionaries in Venice.

B.   **Fill in the blanks.**

7.   Giuseppe Mazzini formed a secret society known as _____.

8.   _____was a young sailor who became Mazzini's right hand man and eventually led the Italians to victory.

9.   _____ became the first king of the nation of Italy in 1861.

10. In 1850, the emperor of China belonged to the _____ dynasty.

11. British merchants brought the drug _____ to Chinese ports.

12. Hong Xiuquan's followers were known as _____.

C. Short Answer. Answer each question using a complete sentence.

13. How did the Italian secret societies disagree about what kind of nation Italy should be?

_____

_____

_____

14. After initially helping the Austrians, why did the French king later agree to fight with the Italians against Austria?

_____

_____

_____

15. By the mid-nineteenth century, why had China become so poor?

_____

_____

_____

16. What did Hong Xiuquan believe about the odd dream he had while studying for his government examination?

_____

_____

_____

17. Why did Hong Xiuquan's followers grow their hair long?

_____

_____

_____

18. Why did the British help fight against the Chinese revolutionaries?

_____

_____

D. Essay. Answer the following question in paragraph form.

19. How did Hong Xiuquan's followers want China to be run?

_____

_____

_____

_____

_____

_____

Name _____ Date _____

Chapter 5 Test: The American Civil War

A. **Sequencing. Number the events in the correct order using 1 for the event that happened first, 6 for the event that happened last, and so on.**

____ President Lincoln announced that the United States would use force to bring the rebel states back into the U.S. After this announcement, four more states joined the rebels.

____ Confederate forces surrendered at Appomattox, Virginia.

____ President Lincoln officially declared that all slaves in the Confederacy would be free.

____ Seven southern states, including South Carolina, Georgia, and Texas, formed the Confederate States of America.

____ Over fifty thousand men were wounded and killed at the Battle of Gettysburg.

____ Confederate soldiers fired on Fort Sumter in South Carolina.

B. **Fill in the blanks.**

7. _____ was the Confederate general who didn't approve of slavery but refused to fight against his home state of Virginia.

8. _____ became President Lincoln's general.

9. President Lincoln's official announcement that all slaves in the Confederacy would be declared free was known as the _____.

10. During the Civil War, hundred of towns and cities were burned and destroyed, including _____.

11. On April 14, 1865, President Lincoln was assassinated by _____.

12. The years after the Civil War were known as a time of _____.

C. **Short Answer. Answer each question using a complete sentence.**

13. Why was slavery so important to the southern states?

_____

_____

_____

14. Why did the northern states not need slaves like the southern states did?

_____

_____

_____

15. How did new states joining the U.S.A. cause a problem?

_____

_____

_____

16. What did President Lincoln's assassination show the country?

_____

_____

_____

17. How did the Thirteenth Amendment to the Constitution change the United States?

_____

_____

_____

D.   Essay. Answer the following question in paragraph form.

18. What were some of the problems that the United States still faced after the Civil War?

_____

_____

_____

_____

_____

_____

The Story of the World

Chapter 6 Test: Two Tries for Freedom

A. **Sequencing. Number the events in the correct order using 1 for the event that happened first, 6 for the event that happened last, and so on.**

_____ Brazilian and Argentinian forces marched into Asunción, the capital city of Paraguay.

_____ Brazil, Argentina, and Uruguay united against Paraguay.

_____ The Paraguayan navy was destroyed by Brazil.

_____ Brazil helped General Flores gain power in Uruguay.

_____ Spanish and Portuguese colonies in South America became independent.

_____ Francisco Solano López marched his army into Argentina.

B. **Fill in the blanks.**

7. Spanish colonists who had been born in South America rather than in Spain were known as _____.

8. Francisco Solano López asked the country of _____ to join with him in a fight against Brazil.

9. The war between Paraguay and Brazil, Argentina, and Uruguay was known as the _____.

10. English-speaking colonists lived in a part of Canada known as Upper Canada, which was later named _____.

11. French-speaking colonists lived in a part of Canada known as Lower Canada, which was later named _____.

12. When the lieutenant-governor of Nova Scotia agreed to let the _____ Assembly choose his advisors, he gave the Assembly the greatest power in the province.

C. Short Answer. Answer each question using a complete sentence.

13. How did Francisco Solano López plan to attack Argentina and Brazil?

_____

_____

_____

14. How were the soldiers of Brazil, Argentina, and Uruguay better prepared for battle than the Paraguayan soldiers?

_____

_____

_____

15. What do the people of Paraguay today think about Francisco Solano López?

_____

_____

_____

16. What did Louis Joseph Papineau encourage the people of Canada to do?

_____

_____

_____

17. What did the Earl of Durham suggest to keep the Canadian provinces from rebelling?

_____

_____

_____

18. What did the British North American Act do?

_____

_____

_____

D.   **Essay. Answer the following question in paragraph form.**

19.   Why did the provinces of Canada argue about forming a federation?

_____

_____

_____

_____

_____

_____

The Story of the World

Chapter 7 Test: Two Empires, Three Republics, and One Kingdom

A. **Sequencing. Number the events in the correct order using 1 for the event that happened first, 6 for the event that happened last, and so on.**

____ Napoleon Bonaparte seized control of the government and crowned himself Emperor.

____ Frenchmen made huge barricades in the streets of Paris during the Three Glorious Days.

____ Louis-Philippe became the Citizen King and reigned for eighteen years.

____ The king and thousands of aristocrats were executed during the French Revolution.

____ The French army was defeated by the Prussians.

____ Louis-Napoleon Bonaparte won the first election for president.

B. **Fill in the blanks.**

7. For many years, kings from the _____ family ruled France.

8. _____ was a Frenchman who helped the American colonists fight for their independence and wanted to see France free from kings as well.

9. _____ was the very last emperor of France.

10. The North German Confederation did not include the state of _____.

11. This new confederation became known as the _____.

12. _____, the third German emperor, was a violent, quarrelsome, quick-tempered bully.

C. **Short Answer. Answer each question using a complete sentence.**

13. What is a constitutional monarchy?

_____

_____

_____

14. Why did Louis-Napoleon take power away from the assembly?

_____

_____

15. What caused the second French Empire to end?

_____

_____

_____

16. What is a confederacy?

_____

_____

_____

17. How did Otto von Bismarck earn the nickname of the "Iron Chancellor?"

_____

_____

_____

18. Why did the German states not allow Wilhelm to call himself the Emperor of Germany?

_____

_____

_____

D. Essay. Answer the following question in paragraph form.

19. Why was Friedrich disturbed by Prussia's overwhelming influence on the German states?

_____

_____

_____

_____

_____

_____

Name _____ Date _____

Chapter 8 Test: Becoming Modern

A. **Sequencing. Number the events in the correct order using 1 for the event that happened first, 6 for the event that happened last, and so on.**

_____ The daimyo, Japanese noblemen, demanded that Yoshinobu resign as shogun and end the Tokugawa shogunate for good.

_____ The samurai revolted when told that they could no longer carry their swords in public.

_____ Matthew Perry convinced Japan to open its ports to American trade.

_____ The revolting samurai were defeated by the new army of peasants with guns.

_____ The daimyo put the seventeen-year-old emperor on the throne of Japan.

_____ Japan adopted a new constitution that made Japan's government much like the German government.

B. **Fill in the blanks.**

7. _____ invented a light powered by electricity and then developed a whole system to run these lights.

8. Before railroads changed the way people kept time, cities all over the world set their own clocks by looking at the _____.

9. _____, a Canadian railroad engineer, suggested that it might be a good idea to divide the world into twenty-four time zones.

10. The Japanese city of Edo was renamed _____ in 1868.

11. Saigo Takamori, a famous samurai warrior, led a rebellion known as the _____.

12. The daimyo who helped the emperor regain his throne called this time period the _____.

C.   Short Answer. Answer each question using a complete sentence.

13.   Before the railroad was built, how would a businessman cross the United States?

_____

_____

_____

14.   What happened at Promontory Summit, Utah, on May 10, 1869?

_____

_____

_____

15.   What did it mean when time became standardized?

_____

_____

_____

16.   Why did Yoshinobu agree to resign as shogun?

_____

_____

_____

17.   How were the conscripts in the new Japanese army different from the samurai?

_____

_____

_____

18.   Under Japan's new constitution, who made the policies for the country?

_____

_____

_____

D. Essay. Answer the following question in paragraph form.

19. How did railroads, time zones, and light bulbs change the United States?

_____

_____

_____

_____

_____

_____

The Story of the World

Chapter 9 Test: Two More Empires, Two Rebellions

A. **Sequencing. Number the events in the correct order using 1 for the event that happened first, 6 for the event that happened last, and so on.**

_____ The Dutch invaded Acheh with three thousand men.

_____ The East Indies became part of the Dutch Empire.

_____ The Dutch government added the kingdom of Acheh to its empire.

_____ Farmers began to revolt against the Dutch government.

_____ The British and Dutch governments made an agreement which allowed the kingdom of Acheh to remain independent.

_____ Tjoet Njak Dien fought with her husband and father against the Dutch.

B. **Fill in the blanks.**

7. The Dutch and the British governments both wanted to claim the island of _____.

8. The people of Acheh fought against the Dutch using _____ warfare, rather than using an organized army on a regular battlefield.

9. Tjoet Njak Dien was a fierce Achenese woman who became known as _____.

10. The Ottoman Empire was ruled by a _____.

11. The Ottoman Empire included the mountainous land north of Greece, which the Turks called the _____, the Turkish word for "mountain."

12. Revolutionaries in _____ revolted against the Turks, but they weren't well organized.

C. Short Answer. Answer each question using a complete sentence.

13. Why was Indonesia once known as the Dutch East Indies?

_____

_____

_____

14. Why was the kingdom of Acheh allowed to remain independent?

_____

_____

_____

15. Why did farmers of the East Indies begin to revolt against the Dutch?

_____

_____

_____

16. What did Abdul Aziz do that shocked the rest of Europe?

_____

_____

_____

17. How did Abdulhamid II try to improve his country?

_____

_____

_____

18. What excuse did the Russian army use to invade the Ottoman Empire?

_____

_____

_____

D. Essay. Answer the following question in paragraph form.

19. Why was the Ottoman Empire known as the "sick man of Europe?"

_____

_____

_____

_____

_____

_____

Name _____   Date _____

Chapter 10 Test: A Canal to the East and a Very Dry Desert

A. **Sequencing. Number the events in the correct order using 1 for the event that happened first, 6 for the event that happened last, and so on.**

_____ Ismail Pasha invited leaders from all over Europe to celebrate the official opening of the new canal.

_____ Muhammad Ali seized the throne of Egypt.

_____ Egyptian army officers led a revolt against the British.

_____ Ismail Pasha sold control of the canal to the British.

_____ Said Pasha gave a French company permission to start digging a canal.

_____ The British captured the Egyptian capital city of Cairo.

B. **Fill in the blanks.**

7.   The _____ Mountains run right down the middle of Peru.

8.   The war between Peru, Bolivia, and Chile was known as the _____.

9.   Admiral Miguel Grau was the commander of the _____, a Peruvian iron warship.

10. Europe and Egypt celebrated when the _____ Canal was completed in 1869.

11. Ismail Pasha was given the title of _____, meaning "king" or "sovereign ruler."

12. When Muhammad Ali seized the throne, Egypt was part of the _____ Empire.

C. **Short Answer. Answer each question using a complete sentence.**

13. Why did Peru help Bolivia in the war against Chile?

_____

_____

_____

14. What happened to Bolivia's coastline after the war with Chile?

_____

_____

_____

15. What happened in Peru after the war with Chile?

_____

_____

_____

16. How did Muhammad Ali try to make Egypt more like the countries of Europe?

_____

_____

_____

17. Why were the countries of Europe so interested in the new canal in Egypt?

_____

_____

_____

18. What did Ismail Pasha do that hurt his country?

_____

_____

_____

D.   Essay. Answer the following question in paragraph form.

19. Describe the Atacama Desert. Why was it so important to both Bolivia and Chile?

_____

_____

_____

_____

_____

The Story of the World

Chapter 11 Test: The Far Parts of the World

A. **Sequencing. Number the events in the correct order using 1 for the event that happened first, 6 for the event that happened last, and so on.**

_____ Ned Kelly was convicted, sentenced, and executed.

_____ The settlements in Australia became regular British colonies.

_____ Gold was discovered in the red Australian earth.

_____ The British colony of Australia became the Commonwealth of Australia.

_____ Ned Kelly's mother, Ellen, was arrested and sent to jail for three years.

_____ Great Britain sent prisoners to Australia because British prisons were overcrowded.

B. **Fill in the blanks.**

7. Bandits known as _____ hid along the roads in Australia, holding up the wagons that took gold from the mines into the towns.

8. When the police finally captured Ned Kelly, he was taken to the city of _____ and put on trial for murder.

9. Leopold II was the king of _____ who wanted his country to grow larger by claiming colonies all around the world.

10. When Leopold began claiming African land for Belgium, the country of _____ quickly followed by claiming lands in both the east and the west of Africa.

11. The years after 1880 became known as _____ because so many countries were trying to gain control of African land.

12. By 1900, _____ and _____ were the only two areas in Africa not claimed by a European country.

C.   Short Answer. Answer each question using a complete sentence.

13.   What did Ned Kelly think about the police in Australia?

_____

_____

_____

14.   What did Australians think about Ned Kelly?

_____

_____

_____

15.   What did it mean when the colony of Australia became the Commonwealth of Australia?

_____

_____

_____

16.   Why were the countries of Europe so interested in Africa?

_____

_____

_____

17.   What was the International African Association?

_____

_____

_____

18.   What was the purpose of the Berlin Conference?

_____

_____

_____

D. Essay. Answer the following question in paragraph form.

19. What were the results of the Berlin Conference?

_____

_____

_____

_____

_____

_____

Name _____ Date _____

The Story of the World

Chapter 12 Test: Unhappy Unions

A. **Sequencing. Number the events in the correct order using 1 for the event that happened first, 6 for the event that happened last, and so on.**

_____ The Afrikaners declared war on the British.

_____ Diamonds were discovered along the banks of the Orange River.

_____ The Boers settled down in two new colonies known as the Free State and Transvaal.

_____ The British government built concentration camps for Afrikaners who lived in areas where guerillas were attacking the British.

_____ The British took over Cape Colony and declared that all slaves would be set free.

_____ The British formed a new colony known as Rhodesia.

B. **Fill in the blanks.**

7. Many Irish farmers grew wheat and oats for their British landlords, but they grew _____ for themselves.

8. _____ was the British Prime Minister who insisted that the Corn Laws should be repealed.

9. _____ was the British Prime Minister who asked Parliament to pass the Home Rule Bill.

10. Along with diamonds, huge deposits of _____ were found in South Africa.

11. The British called the war between Great Britain and the Afrikaners the _____ War.

12. When the British finally set the people of _____ free, the tide of the battle had turned, and the Afrikaners began to surrender.

C. Short Answer. Answer each question using a complete sentence.

13. Why had the Irish not gotten along with the English for so many years?

_____

_____

_____

14. What were the Corn Laws?

_____

_____

_____

15. What was the Home Rule Bill?

_____

_____

_____

16. Why did the Boers begin to call themselves Afrikaners?

_____

_____

_____

17. Why did the Afrikaners declare war on Great Britain?

_____

_____

_____

18. What was the result of the treaty known as the Peace of Vereeniging?

_____

_____

_____

D. Essay. Answer the following question in paragraph form.

19. What was the blight? Why did it affect Ireland so greatly?

_____

_____

_____

_____

_____

_____

Name _____ Date _____

Chapter 13 Test: The Old-Fashioned Emperor and the Red Sultan

A. **Sequencing. Number the events in the correct order using 1 for the event that happened first, 6 for the event that happened last, and so on.**

_____ Abdulhamid II organized a huge spy network to listen for any talk of rebellion or revolt.

_____ Abdulhamid II dissolved the Ottoman constitution.

_____ Ottoman soldiers killed over a hundred thousand Armenians and forced others to leave their homes.

_____ The Armenians rebelled against the Ottoman Empire.

_____ University students began to plot to change the laws of the Ottoman Empire.

_____ Ottoman Turks living in Geneva and Paris began to organize into a movement to change the Ottoman Empire and get rid of Abdulhamid II.

B. **Fill in the blanks.**

7. The first emperor of Brazil, Pedro I, was the son of the king of _____.

8. Pedro II agreed with his father that _____ was a "cancer" on Brazil and should be outlawed.

9. At the end of Pedro's reign, many Brazilians believed that Brazil should be a _____ with a constitution of its own.

10. Abdulhamid II became known as Abdulhamid the _____ because he had shed so much blood.

11. A group of medical students wanted to change the Ottoman Empire and the way it was ruled and form a new country known as _____.

12. These students were known as the _____.

C. Short Answer. Answer each question using a complete sentence.

13. What five groups of people lived in Brazil during the reign of Pedro II?

_____

_____

_____

14. Why did the Council of State tell Pedro II that he should leave the country?

_____

_____

_____

15. What do Brazilians today think about Pedro II?

_____

_____

_____

16. What did Article 113 of the Turkish constitution say?

_____

_____

_____

17. Why were the Armenians not treated well by the Ottomans?

_____

_____

_____

18. How did the medical students at Istanbul University and other colleges want to change the Ottoman Empire?

_____

_____

_____

D. Essay. Answer the following question in paragraph form.

19. What did Pedro II do to help Brazil prosper?

_____

_____

_____

_____

_____

Name _____ Date _____

Chapter 14 Test: Two Czars and Two Emperors

A. **Sequencing. Number the events in the correct order using 1 for the event that happened first, 6 for the event that happened last, and so on.**

_____ Menelik signed a treaty with the Italians giving Italy a tiny coastal area as a colony.

_____ Even though they were polite to each other, and even made a deal to fight off invaders together, Yohannes and Menelik plotted against each other and made deals with Italian and British army officers to get more weapons.

_____ Yohannes was shot during a battle against invaders from the west.

_____ Both Yohannes and Menelik claimed that, by right, he was the emperor of Ethiopia and deserved the title "King of Kings."

_____ Italy, Great Britain, and France all signed treaties recognizing Ethiopia's independence.

_____ Menelik defeated the Italians at the Battle of Adowa.

B. **Fill in the blanks.**

7. Alexander II belonged to the royal _____ family of Russia.

8. Russians who spoke out against Alexander III were sent to _____.

9. When Alexander III died, his son, _____, became czar.

10. By the 1880's, _____ and Ethiopia were the only two African countries free from European rule.

11. Yohannes IV and Menelik II both argued over who deserved the traditional Ethiopian title _____.

12. After the Battle of Adowa, Menelik earned the title _____.

C. Short Answer. Answer each question using a complete sentence.

13. What did Alexander III do as soon as he became czar?

_____

_____

_____

14. What were two ways that Alexander II tried to make Russia more Western?

_____

_____

_____

15. What was life like for the Jews of Russia?

_____

_____

_____

16. How did the Italians trick Menelik?

_____

_____

_____

17. What caused the Italian defeat at the Battle of Adowa?

_____

_____

_____

18. Why did Italy, Great Britain, and France all sign treaties recognizing Ethiopia's independence?

_____

_____

_____

D. Essay. Answer the following question in paragraph form.

19. It is said of Alexander III that he "set out to undo everything that his father did." How did he do this?

_____

_____

_____

_____

_____

_____

Name _____ Date _____

Chapter 15 Test: Small Countries with Large Invaders

A. Sequencing. Number the events in the correct order using 1 for the event that happened first, 6 for the event that happened last, and so on.

_____ José Rizal published his novel, *Touch Me Not*.

_____ America declared war on Spain and began attacking the Spanish navy all over the world.

_____ Spain surrendered, and America and Spain signed the Treaty of Paris.

_____ Cuban revolutionaries began to fight for their independence.

_____ The president of the Philippines declared war on the United States.

_____ A United States battleship called the *Maine* blew up in a Cuban harbor.

B. Fill in the blanks.

7. King Kojong was the king of Korea, but many people believed his wife, _____, was the real ruler.

8. The Sino-Japanese War took place in _____.

9. Cuba was important to Spain because so many fields of _____ grew there.

10. _____ and _____ were two American newspaper owners who published exaggerated stories about the Cuban crisis.

11. _____ was the Assistant Secretary of the Navy who helped direct the U.S. battleships during the Spanish-American War.

12. He also led a band of soldiers nicknamed the _____ in a famous battle up San Juan Hill.

C. Short Answer. Answer each question using a complete sentence.

13. Why did Korea become known as the "Hermit Country?"

_____

_____

_____

14. What happened to China at the end of the Sino-Japanese War?

_____

_____

_____

15. What happened when the Queen of Korea asked the Russians to become Korea's ally?

_____

_____

_____

16. What was the hidden message in José Rizal's novel, *Touch Me Not*?

_____

_____

_____

17. Why were American newspapers so eager for the United States to declare war on Spain?

_____

_____

_____

18. What happened as a result of the Treaty of Paris?

_____

_____

_____

D. **Essay. Answer the following question in paragraph form.**

19.   Explain the events that caused the Sino-Japanese War.

_____

_____

_____

_____

_____

_____

Name _____ Date _____

Chapter 16 Test: The Expanding United States

A. **Sequencing. Number the events in the correct order using 1 for the event that happened first, 6 for the event that happened last, and so on.**

_____ The U.S. government sent soldiers to drive the Native Americans off their land.

_____ Government officials wanted those people moving west to claim the land for the U.S. government, so they traveled west and divided the land into areas called territories.

_____ More and more people from cities along the East Coast started to move to the western part of the U.S. because the cities were filling up.

_____ Native Americans began to defend their villages and hunting grounds against the pioneers.

_____ American businessmen built railroads that crisscrossed the country.

_____ The buffalo became an endangered species.

B. **Fill in the blanks.**

7. The government marked off certain areas of land called _____ where the Native Americans were forced to live.

8. _____ was a Lakota chief who gathered a group of warriors to fight back against the U.S. soldiers.

9. _____ was an Apache chief who also fought against the U.S. soldiers in the New Mexico and Arizona territories.

10. A _____ invests money in a company and then gets a share of the profits at the end of the year.

11. A _____ is a business in which more than one person has the right to share in the profits.

12. A _____ gives away money for the good of others.

C. Short Answer. Answer each question using a complete sentence.

13. Why did so many Americans decide to move west?

_____

_____

_____

14. How did a western territory become a state?

_____

_____

_____

15. What happened at the Battle of Little Bighorn?

_____

_____

_____

16. Why did people have to stop selling goods that they made in their homes?

_____

_____

_____

17. What did these home workers have to do?

_____

_____

_____

18. What did Andrew Carnegie do with the money he made?

_____

_____

_____

D. **Essay. Answer the following question in paragraph form.**

19. What did Andrew Carnegie believe about the poor and the rich?

_____

_____

_____

_____

_____

_____

Name _____   Date _____

The Story of the World

Chapter 17 Test: China's Troubles

A. **Sequencing. Number the events in the correct order using 1 for the event that happened first, 6 for the event that happened last, and so on.**

_____ The Russian forces at Port Arthur had to surrender to the Japanese.

_____ The Japanese broke off diplomatic relations with Russia.

_____ Japanese diplomats requested that Russia remove her troops from Port Arthur.

_____ Japanese destroyers launched a surprise attack against the Russian navy.

_____ Russian soldiers were defeated at the Battle of Mukden, the largest land battle ever fought up to this time.

_____ Russian and Japanese soldiers fought together during the Boxer Rebellion.

B. **Fill in the blanks.**

7. During the Boxer Rebellion, Guangxu was emperor of China, but _____ was the real ruler with all of the power.

8. The Chinese government had its headquarters in the _____ inside Beijing.

9. The Boxers attacked the legation compound in Beijing where many foreign countries had offices known as _____.

10. After the Boxer Rebellion, Russia decided to seize the country of _____.

11. The commander of the Japanese navy was _____.

12. American President _____ helped to arrange a peace treaty between Russia and Japan.

C.   Short Answer. Answer each question using a complete sentence.

13.   How did the Emperor Guangxu make himself unpopular with so many Chinese?

_____

_____

_____

14.   Why did the Boxers pull up railway lines in China?

_____

_____

_____

15.   What was the result of the Boxer Rebellion?

_____

_____

_____

16.   Why was Port Arthur so important to the Russians?

_____

_____

_____

17.   Why were the Russians confident that Japan would not attack them?

_____

_____

_____

18.   What did the war between Russia and Japan show the world?

_____

_____

_____

D. Essay. Answer the following question in paragraph form.

19. Who were the Boxers? What was their goal? How did they plan to accomplish this goal?

_____

_____

_____

_____

_____

_____

The Story of the World

Chapter 18 Test: Europe and the Countries Just East

A. **Sequencing. Number the events in the correct order using 1 for the event that happened first, 6 for the event that happened last, and so on.**

_____ The Young Turks forced Abdulhamid to bring back the Turkish constitution.

_____ France, Germany, Great Britain, and Austria split Bulgaria into two parts—a northern part ruled by a Russian prince and a southern part that would belong to the Turks.

_____ Albania won its independence from the Ottoman Turks.

_____ Macedonian rebels declared themselves independent of Turkish rule.

_____ The sultan Abdulhamid ordered Turkish soldiers to march into Macedonia and kill the rebels.

_____ The northern and southern parts of Bulgaria reunited.

B. **Fill in the blanks.**

7. In 1906, Persians began rioting in the streets of _____, the capital of Persia, because they wanted a constitution that would limit the shah's power.

8. The shah finally agreed to the people's demands, and the National Consultative Assembly, or the _____, was created to help rule the country.

9. The _____ Peninsula in Eastern Europe includes Greece, Bulgaria, and several other small countries.

10. When Macedonian rebels joined together in Krusevo and declared themselves free from Turkish rule, it became known as the _____ Uprising.

11. The Young Turks wanted to get rid of _____ laws and have secular laws instead.

12. Bulgaria made an alliance with _____ that caused Serbia to become more and more hostile to both of these countries.

C. Short Answer. Answer each question using a complete sentence.

13. What did Mozaffar od-Din Shah sell to William Knox D'Arcy?

_____

_____

_____

14. Why did Great Britain and Russia have so much power over Persia?

_____

_____

_____

15. How did Mohammad Ali Shah try to take stronger control of his own country, so that he could better deal with Great Britain and Russia? How did the Persian people react?

_____

_____

_____

16. What did Abdulhamid do that made him unpopular with the Ottoman army and people?

_____

_____

_____

17. What did the Young Turks' Proclamation for the Ottoman Empire say?

_____

_____

_____

18. Why didn't Macedonia and Albania want to be a part of an Ottoman nation?

_____

_____

_____

D. Essay. Answer the following question in paragraph form.

19. Why were the British so interested in Persia?

_____

_____

_____

_____

_____

_____

The Story of the World

Chapter 19 Test: China, Vietnam—and France

A. **Sequencing. Number the events in the correct order using 1 for the event that happened first, 6 for the event that happened last, and so on.**

_____ Phan Boi Chau fled to Japan but was ordered to leave by the Japanese government.

_____ Phan Boi Chau was offered a job in the Vietnamese government.

_____ Phan Boi Chau was arrested by the Chinese and placed in jail.

_____ Phan Boi Chau formed a group called the Restoration Society and convinced a Vietnamese prince to join it.

_____ Phan Boi Chau was tried for treason and convicted in Vietnam.

_____ Phan Boi Chau began to doubt that the Vietnamese would ever be able to get the French out of their country.

B. **Fill in the blanks.**

7. _____ was the last emperor of China.

8. Sun Yixian was the head of a group of revolutionaries who called themselves the _____.

9. The capital of the new Chinese republic was the city of _____.

10. The countries of Vietnam, Laos, and Cambodia are located on a peninsula known as _____.

11. For hundreds of years, the _____ dynasty of emperors had ruled Vietnam.

12. The French divided their territory in Vietnam into three colonies known as _____, _____, and _____.

C. Short Answer. Answer each question using a complete sentence.

13. During the reign of the last emperor, who really controlled China?

_____

_____

_____

14. What caused the people of the Sichuan Province to revolt?

_____

_____

_____

15. What happened to the last emperor of China?

_____

_____

_____

16. Why were the Vietnamese unhappy with the French?

_____

_____

_____

17. Why were the rebellions organized by Phan Boi Chau and the Vietnamese Restoration Society unsuccessful?

_____

_____

_____

18. What do the Vietnamese think about Phan Boi Chau today?

_____

_____

_____

D. Essay. Answer the following question in paragraph form.

19. What were Sun Yixian's Three Principles of the People?

_____

_____

_____

_____

_____

_____

Name _____ Date _____

Chapter 20 Test: Revolution in the Americas...War in the World

A. Sequencing. Number the events in the correct order using 1 for the event that happened first, 6 for the event that happened last, and so on.

_____ Great Britain declared war on Germany.

_____ Germany marched through Belgium and headed towards France.

_____ Archduke Franz Ferdinand was shot by a nineteen-year old assassin from Serbia.

_____ The United States declared war on Germany.

_____ The Austro-Hungarian Empire declared war on Serbia.

_____ A German submarine fired a torpedo and sank the *Lusitania*.

B. Fill in the blanks.

7. _____, a cattle thief and bandit, became a guerilla warrior who fought against the Mexican government.

8. _____ was the leader of a group of rebels who removed President Madero from office.

9. For many years, the people of Europe called World War I _____ .

10. During World War I, Austria, Germany, Bulgaria, and the Ottoman Turks were known as the _____.

11. Great Britain, France, Russia, and a collection of other countries were called the _____.

12. During World War I, Great Britain passed a new law called the _____, which allowed the government to order men to join the army even if they didn't want to.

C.   Short Answer. Answer each question using a complete sentence.

13.   Why was Porfirio Díaz the president of Mexico for so long?

_____

_____

_____

14.   When Francisco Madero ran against Porfirio Díaz, what happened?

_____

_____

_____

15.   What happened during the Ten Tragic Days?

_____

_____

_____

16.   Why did the British begin to worry when the Germans marched through Belgium?

_____

_____

_____

17.   Why was the rest of the world so furious when the Germans sank the *Lusitania*?

_____

_____

_____

18.   What caused the United States to enter World War I?

_____

_____

_____

D. Essay. Answer the following question in paragraph form.

19. What problems did Francisco Madero face when he finally became president of Mexico?

_____

_____

_____

_____

_____

_____

The Story of the World

Chapter 21 Test: A Revolution Begins, and the Great War Ends

A. **Sequencing. Number the events in the correct order using 1 for the event that happened first, 6 for the event that happened last, and so on.**

_____ Nicholas II gave up his throne, and the Provisional Government began ruling Russia.

_____ The czar and his family were killed.

_____ Nicholas II took over control of the Russian army.

_____ The Bolsheviks seized control of the government.

_____ Almost two million Russian soldiers deserted the army and marched home.

_____ The Russian army entered World War I.

B. **Fill in the blanks.**

7. _____ was a strange, mystical monk who claimed that he could heal the czar's son, who suffered from hemophilia.

8. _____ was the leader of the Provisional Government in Russia.

9. Vladimir Ilich Lenin was the leader of the Bolsheviks who took over the Russian government and renamed themselves the _____.

10. _____ was the President of the United States during World War I.

11. During World War I, American soldiers were nicknamed _____.

12. Women who marched, protested, and spoke in public about their right to vote were called _____.

C. Short Answer. Answer each question using a complete sentence.

13. What problem did the Russian army face when they entered World War I?

_____

_____

_____

14. Why did Lenin think that peasants had the right to take over land owned by the wealthy?

_____

_____

_____

15. Why did the Bolsheviks rename some of Russia's cities?

_____

_____

_____

16. Why did the president think that the United States had to join World War I?

_____

_____

_____

17. How did American women help during World War I?

_____

_____

_____

18. How did World War I show that women should be allowed to vote?

_____

_____

_____

D. Essay. Answer the following question in paragraph form.

19. How did Lenin tackle Russian poverty? What was the problem with his idea?

_____

_____

_____

_____

_____

_____

The Story of the World

Chapter 22 Test: National Uprisings

A. Sequencing. Number the events in the correct order using 1 for the event that happened first, 6 for the event that happened last, and so on.

____ Resistance groups such as Sinn Féin, the Fenians, and the Irish Land League began to form in Ireland.

____ Sinn Féin signed a treaty with the British government that created the Irish Free State.

____ Protestants in the northern part of Ireland signed a document that promised they would fight back if the British government gave Ireland home rule.

____ Four hundred people died during the Easter Uprising.

____ The British government allowed the Irish Free State to become a completely independent country called the Republic of Ireland.

____ Sinn Féin set up its own government called the Dáil Éireann or the Irish Assembly.

B. Fill in the blanks.

7. Members of the _____ League hoped that the Irish would be able to abandon speaking English, in favor of the ancient Irish language.

8. The six counties in the northern part of Ireland were called _____.

9. A Sinn Féin leader named Michael Collins organized his own army called the _____.

10. The British called India the _____, the Indian name for kingdom.

11. The British moved the capital of India to _____.

12. The _____ Party, led by Mohandas Gandhi, called for Indian independence from Great Britain.

C. Short Answer. Answer each question using a complete sentence.

13. Why did many of the Irish in the northern part of Ireland oppose home rule?

_____

_____

_____

14. What happened during the Easter Uprising?

_____

_____

_____

15. What did the treaty between Sinn Féin and the British government say?

_____

_____

_____

16. How did the British try to improve life in India?

_____

_____

_____

17. What happened when demonstrators met in Amritsar to protest against British rule?

_____

_____

_____

18. What is satyagraha?

_____

_____

_____

D. Essay. Answer the following question in paragraph form.

19. What were some of the things Gandhi and his followers did to resist British rule?

_____

_____

_____

_____

_____

_____

The Story of the World

Chapter 23 Test: "Peace" and a Man of War

A.   **Sequencing. Number the events in the correct order using 1 for the event that happened first, 6 for the event that happened last, and so on.**

_____ Lenin had a stroke, and Joseph Stalin became the real leader of Russia.

_____ A million and a half Russians who had supported the czar and the White Army were forced to leave their country; those who didn't leave were arrested, jailed, or executed.

_____ A drought spread across Russia, and crops began to wither and die.

_____ Joseph Stalin told the countries at the western border of Russia that they had to become part of a new communist empire.

_____ After Nicholas II and his family were killed, civil war broke out in Russia between Russians loyal to the czar and the communists.

_____ Six million Russians starved to death.

B.   **Fill in the blanks.**

7.   After World War I had finally ended, the leaders of the victorious countries met at the palace built by Louis XIV at _____.

8.   The peace settlement signed at this conference created a new country called _____ that included Croatia, Bosnia, Serbia, and Montenegro.

9.   Austria and Hungary became two separate countries, and a big slice of land across the top of both was taken away and made into a new country called _____.

10.   During the civil war, Russians who were loyal to the czar formed the _____ Army while the communists formed the _____ Army.

11.   Joseph Stalin had the city of Petrograd renamed _____.

12.   Anyone who muttered about Stalin's cruelty was shot or sent to _____.

C. Short Answer. Answer each question using a complete sentence.

13. What was the League of Nations?

_____

_____

_____

14. What did Article 231 of the peace settlement say?

_____

_____

_____

15. What problem did the new countries created by the peace settlement face?

_____

_____

_____

16. What is a totalitarian state?

_____

_____

_____

17. How did Joseph Stalin plan to make Russia great?

_____

_____

_____

18. What were collective farms?

_____

_____

_____

D.   Essay. Answer the following question in paragraph form.

19.   Who were the three most powerful leaders who met at the conference following the end of World War I? What did each of these leaders think the peace treaty should do?

_____

_____

_____

_____

_____

_____

Name _____   Date _____

The Story of the World

Chapter 24 Test: The King and Il Duce

A.   **Sequencing. Number the events in the correct order using 1 for the event that happened first, 6 for the event that happened last, and so on.**

_____ Three Egyptian patriots requested permission to travel to London on a diplomatic visit, but were imprisoned instead.

_____ At the beginning of World War I, Great Britain announced that Egypt would no longer have any relationship with the Ottoman Empire and declared that Egypt was under martial law.

_____ Great Britain formally granted Egypt its freedom.

_____ Riots broke out in Cairo, and fighting erupted between armed Egyptians and British soldiers.

_____ Ahmad Fu'ad was publicly declared King Fu'ad I of Egypt.

_____ 'Abbas II, the khedive of Egypt, fled to Vienna, Austria.

B.   **Fill in the blanks.**

7.   After 'Abbas II fled to Vienna, Egypt was ruled by a _____ instead of a khedive.

8.   The national movement for Egyptian independence was known as _____.

9.   _____ was the first king of an independent Egypt.

10. At the Versailles peace talks, Italy was hoping to get some of the land that lay along the _____.

11. Mussolini's followers were called _____ after a bundle of sticks with an axe in its center that was a symbol of the ancient Roman government.

12. Mussolini was nicknamed _____.

C. **Short Answer. Answer each question using a complete sentence.**

13. Why was Egypt so important to Great Britain?

_____

_____

_____

14. After Britain granted Egypt its freedom, what kind of government did Egypt have?

_____

_____

_____

15. Who was involved in the three-way struggle for power in Egypt?

_____

_____

_____

16. What did Mussolini think was the most important thing for any country?

_____

_____

_____

17. Why were Italians so eager to listen to Mussolini?

_____

_____

_____

18. What was Mussolini's ultimate goal for Italy?

_____

_____

_____

D.   Essay. Answer the following question in paragraph form.

19.   Why didn't Italy's prime minister help write the treaty that ended World War I?

_____

_____

_____

_____

_____

_____

The Story of the World

Chapter 25 Test: Armies in China

A. **Sequencing. Number the events in the correct order using 1 for the event that happened first, 6 for the event that happened last, and so on.**

_____ Sun Yixian was forced to hand over power to a warlord named Yuan Shikai.

_____ The National Revolutionary Army took control of Beijing and the Chinese government.

_____ Chiang Kai-shek traveled to the Soviet Union to see how the Red Army worked.

_____ The Japanese army invaded and captured Chinese towns all over Manchuria.

_____ Japan demanded that Yuan Shikai give the Chinese provinces of Manchuria, Shantung and Inner Mongolia to the Japanese.

_____ Hirohito ascended the Japanese throne.

B. **Fill in the blanks.**

7. Sun Yixian organized a group of followers into a political party called the _____, or the Kuomintang.

8. After the Japanese army had captured Chinese towns all over Manchuria, they announced that it was a new country known as _____.

9. The Japanese army promised to make _____ the emperor of this new Japanese Empire in China.

10. Representatives of the Russian Communist Party drew up a _____, or statement of beliefs, that the Chinese communists could use.

11. One of the first members of the Chinese Communist Party was _____, who later became its most powerful leader.

12. This leader and his followers settled on the edge of the Jiangxi province and announced that their community was a new nation called the _____.

C. Short Answer. Answer each question using a complete sentence.

13. When Yuan Shikai took over the Chinese government, who did he have to fight off to keep his power?

_____

_____

_____

14. Why did Sun Yixian and Chiang Kai-shek ask Russia to send help?

_____

_____

_____

15. Why didn't Hirohito order the Japanese army to leave Manchuria?

_____

_____

_____

16. Why did many Chinese think that the Soviet Union was a good model for a new China?

_____

_____

_____

17. What did Chiang Kai-shek think about the Chinese Communist Party?

_____

_____

_____

18. What was the Long March?

_____

_____

_____

D. Essay. Answer the following question in paragraph form.

19. Why was Chiang Kai-shek forced to make peace with the Chinese Communist Party?

_____

_____

_____

_____

_____

_____

Name _____ Date _____

Chapter 26 Test: The Great Crash, and What Came of It

A.   **Sequencing. Number the events in the correct order using 1 for the event that happened first, 6 for the event that happened last, and so on.**

____ Germany borrowed huge amounts of money from American and British banks.

____ The American stock market crashed.

____ Adolf Hitler traveled through Germany promising to bring order, wealth, and greatness to Germany.

____ Adolf Hitler was elected German chancellor.

____ Germany was forced to sign the Peace of Versailles.

____ People in Germany began to lose their jobs, and more and more businesses folded.

B.   **Fill in the blanks.**

7.   In the United States, people who wanted to buy and sell parts of companies all met together in an area of New York City called _____.

8.   In the 1930s, during the time period known as the _____, many Americans had very little money to spend.

9.   During the 1930s, when huge droughts killed hundreds of thousands of acres of crops, the middle part of America became known as the _____.

10. After World War I, Germany was forced to pay _____, huge sums of money to make up for all the money France and Britain had spent during the war.

11. Members of the National Socialist German Workers' Party became known as _____.

12. Hitler blamed the _____ for most of Germany's problems.

C. Short Answer. Answer each question using a complete sentence.

13. What is the stock market?

_____

_____

_____

14. What was the Reconstruction Finance Corporation?

_____

_____

_____

15. What did Franklin Roosevelt do to help give Americans jobs and salaries?

_____

_____

_____

16. What did Hitler think about Germany and German culture?

_____

_____

_____

17. Why was anti-Semitism so widespread in many European countries?

_____

_____

_____

18. Why were the Germans so willing to listen to Hitler?

_____

_____

D. Essay. Answer the following question in paragraph form.

19. What are some of the factors that led to the stock market crash?

_____

_____

_____

_____

_____

_____

The Story of the World

Chapter 27 Test: Civil War and Invasion

A. Sequencing. Number the events in the correct order using 1 for the event that happened first, 6 for the event that happened last, and so on.

_____ The Spanish army called itself the Nationalist Party of Spain, and made Francisco Franco their leader.

_____ Monarchists, Republicans, and independence fighters began fighting in the streets.

_____ Alfonso XIII died in Rome.

_____ Spain held elections for a Spanish Parliament and president.

_____ Countries such as the United States, Italy, Germany, and the Soviet Union took sides during the Spanish Civil War.

_____ Alfonso XIII, afraid that civil war was coming, left Spain and went to Rome.

B. Fill in the blanks.

7. Revolutionaries who wanted to see the end of the monarchy in Spain were known as _____.

8. Wealthy, aristocratic Spaniards who wanted Spain to stay a monarchy were called citizens of _____.

9. People in _____ insisted that they should be a free country, independent from Spain.

10. The German takeover of _____ was known as the Anschluss.

11. Great Britain worked out an agreement with Hitler that allowed Germany to have the western half of Czechoslovakia called the _____.

12. When war was finally declared, Germany, Italy, and their allies were known as the _____, and the armies fighting against them, including Great Britain and France, were known as the _____.

C. Short Answer. Answer each question using a complete sentence.

13. What happened when Spain sent its army to stop a revolt in Morocco?

_____

_____

_____

14. What two sides fought during the Spanish Civil War? What did each side want?

_____

_____

_____

15. When Francisco Franco gained power over the whole country, how did he keep control?

_____

_____

_____

16. Why didn't Great Britain and France try to stop Hitler when he broke the Treaty of Versailles by building up his army?

_____

_____

_____

17. What deal did Hitler make with Joseph Stalin?

_____

_____

_____

18. What caused Great Britain and France to finally declare war on Hitler?

_____

_____

_____

D. Essay. Answer the following question in paragraph form.

19. What was Hitler's plan for taking over Europe?

_____

_____

_____

_____

_____

_____

Name _____   Date _____

Chapter 28 Test: The Second World War

A. **Sequencing. Number the events in the correct order using 1 for the event that happened first, 6 for the event that happened last, and so on.**

_____ Japanese fighter planes bombed the U.S. fleet anchored at Pearl Harbor in Hawaii.

_____ Japan took over Hong Kong, the Philippine Islands, and Malaya.

_____ The Japanese attacked the Marco Polo Bridge outside of Beijing, and the Second Sino-Japanese War began.

_____ The United States declared war on Japan, Germany, and Italy.

_____ The Kuomintang government and the Chinese Communist Party made an alliance to fight against the Japanese.

_____ Japan declared itself an Axis power, along with Germany and Italy.

B. **Fill in the blanks.**

7. When World War II began, _____ was the president of the United States.

8. _____ was the emperor of Japan during World War II.

9. In the Battle of _____, four huge Japanese aircraft carriers were destroyed by a much smaller American force.

10. Hitler believed that _____, people with German blood, were smarter, stronger, and better than other people.

11. When _____, an African-American, won four gold medals at the 1936 Olympics, Hitler refused to acknowledge him.

12. The only country to act officially in protection of the Jews was _____, which rounded up all of the Jews living there and helped them get to a safer country.

C. Short Answer. Answer each question using a complete sentence.

13. Why did Japan declare itself to be an Axis power?

_____

_____

_____

14. Before the Japanese attacked, how was the United States involved in the war?

_____

_____

_____

15. Why did Japan attack the U.S. fleet at Pearl Harbor?

_____

_____

_____

16. What were Jews forced to wear in every territory claimed by the Germans?

_____

_____

_____

17. What was Kristallnacht?

_____

_____

_____

18. What is one way people tried to help the Jews?

_____

_____

D. **Essay. Answer the following question in paragraph form.**

19. What was Hitler's "final solution" for the "problem" of the Jews in Europe?

_____

_____

_____

_____

_____

_____

Name _____ Date _____

Chapter 29 Test: The End of World War II

A. **Sequencing. Number the events in the correct order using 1 for the event that happened first, 6 for the event that happened last, and so on.**

_____ Nazis took control of Paris and northern France.

_____ German soldiers marched into Russia and reached the edges of the city of Moscow.

_____ Soviet soldiers invaded Finland, and German soldiers invaded Denmark.

_____ The German and British air forces fought for two months in the Battle of Britain.

_____ Germany officially surrendered on V-E Day.

_____ Allied forces in France retreated to Dunkirk where they planned to sail across the English Channel to safety.

B. **Fill in the blanks.**

7. The area in the south of France where some of the French agreed to cooperate with the Nazis became known as _____.

8. The Allied troops were under the command of American General _____ when they managed to capture the beaches at Normandy.

9. On December 16, 1944, the German army launched the biggest attack the American soldiers had ever seen in what became known as the _____.

10. _____ was a German scientist who had been studying how atoms worked, but he left Germany because he was a Jew.

11. President _____ decided to use an atomic bomb to force the Japanese to surrender.

12. The first atomic bomb was dropped on the Japanese city of _____.

C. Short Answer. Answer each question using a complete sentence.

13. What was the Blitzkrieg?

_____

_____

_____

14. What did Winston Churchill call the "worst evil" faced by the British forces?

_____

_____

_____

15. What was D-Day?

_____

_____

_____

16. What was the Manhattan Project?

_____

_____

_____

17. After World War II was finally over, what organization was formed?

_____

_____

_____

18. What was the most pressing job of this new organization?

_____

_____

_____

D. Essay. Answer the following question in paragraph form.

19. Why is the decision to use the atomic bomb still so controversial?

_____

_____

_____

_____

_____

_____

Name _____ Date _____

Chapter 30 Test: Partitioned Countries

A. Sequencing. Number the events in the correct order using 1 for the event that happened first, 6 for the event that happened last, and so on.

_____ Three hundred unarmed Indians were killed by British soldiers in the city of Amritsar.

_____ World War II swept across the world, and Indians had to put off their wish for independence.

_____ Thousands of people were killed in riots between Hindus and Muslims.

_____ The Muslim League demanded that the British and Hindus agree to separate off part of India for Muslims to rule.

_____ Gandhi was assassinated by Nathuram Vinayak Godse.

_____ India was declared independent.

B. Fill in the blanks.

7. Gandhi's Congress Party became known as the _____.

8. At the same time as India was finally granted its independence, the country of _____ was born.

9. For many years, this new nation and India argued and fought over a piece of land called _____, just north of India.

10. The idea that there should be a Jewish country was called _____.

11. In 1947, the _____ voted to create the nation of Israel.

12. _____ had been living in the land of Palestine for one thousand years.

C. Short Answer. Answer each question using a complete sentence.

13. What did Muslims dislike about the Hindu religion?

_____

_____

_____

14. Why did fifteen million Indians leave their homes after India gained independence?

_____

_____

_____

15. Why did Nathuram Vinayak Godse assassinate Gandhi?

_____

_____

_____

16. What caused both Jews and non-Jews to become more interested in the idea of a Jewish homeland?

_____

_____

_____

17. Who attacked Israel on the very day that independence was declared?

_____

_____

_____

18. What was the outcome of this war?

_____

_____

_____

D. Essay. Answer the following question in paragraph form.

19. Why did creating the nation of Israel cause such a problem?

_____

_____

_____

_____

_____

Name _____   Date _____

The Story of the World

Chapter 31 Test: Western Bullies and American Money

A.   **Sequencing. Number the events in the correct order using 1 for the event that happened first, 6 for the event that happened last, and so on.**

_____ The Israeli army marched into Egyptian territory.

_____ Nasser closed the Suez Canal.

_____ The United Nations ordered Great Britain and France to leave Egypt alone.

_____ Ninety army officers, led by Nasser, took over the Egyptian government.

_____ French and British soldiers arrived at the city of Port Said and began fighting.

_____ The United States Congress passed the Eisenhower Doctrine.

B.   **Fill in the blanks.**

7.   Nasser hoped to unite all of the Arabs in the world into a powerful country that would be known as the _____.

8.   When Nasser decided to close the Suez Canal, it became known as the _____.

9.   The president of the United States during this time was _____.

10. George Marshall was the _____, an advisor to the president whose job is to help America keep its friendship with other countries around the world.

11. A movie called *The Home We Love* was about a small town in southern _____ that was shattered by the war but slowly rebuilt.

12. In 1961 a huge fence was built that divided the city of _____ in half, and no one was allowed to cross the fence without government permission.

C. Short Answer. Answer each question using a complete sentence.

13. What made Nasser so angry that he closed the Suez Canal?

_____

_____

_____

14. Why did Israeli troops invade Egypt?

_____

_____

_____

15. What was the Eisenhower Doctrine?

_____

_____

_____

16. Why did countries in Europe need help after World War II?

_____

_____

_____

17. What was the Marshall Plan?

_____

_____

_____

18. Why did Joseph Stalin refuse to accept help from the United States?

_____

_____

_____

D. Essay. Answer the following question in paragraph form.

19. What happened to Germany after World War II?

_____

_____

_____

_____

_____

_____

Name _____ Date _____

Chapter 32 Test: Africa and China After World War II

A. **Sequencing. Number the events in the correct order using 1 for the event that happened first, 6 for the event that happened last, and so on.**

_____ The Chinese Communist Party's soldiers captured the city of Nanjing.

_____ British and American soldiers came to China to fight against the Japanese.

_____ Mao became the chairman of the new communist nation of China.

_____ Kuomintang soldiers began to switch sides.

_____ The Chinese Communist Party and the Kuomintang began to fight between themselves for control of China's government.

_____ China began to grow more prosperous.

B. **Fill in the blanks.**

7. Black Africans gathered together into a group called the _____, to gain more rights for blacks in South Africa.

8. _____ agreed with Hitler's views about how superior white civilization was to any other culture, and they formed the National Party.

9. When the National Party passed laws that separated whites from the rest of South Africa, it was known as _____.

10. The Chinese Communist Party's soldiers were known as the _____.

11. When the communist army forced the Kuomintang government out of Nanjing, they fled south to the island of _____.

12. China's official name under the communists was _____.

C. Short Answer. Answer each question using a complete sentence.

13. Who did the National Party think should control the government of South Africa?

_____

_____

_____

14. How did black South Africans protest the Unjust Laws passed by the Nationalist Party?

_____

_____

_____

15. How did the South African government respond to these protests?

_____

_____

_____

16. Why did millions of Chinese join the Chinese Communist Party?

_____

_____

_____

17. What problem did the Kuomintang have with its army?

_____

_____

_____

18. After gaining power, what did Mao and the communists do with the people who still supported the Kuomintang?

_____

_____

_____

D. Essay. Answer the following question in paragraph form.

19. What were some of the "acts" passed by the National Party in South Africa?

_____

_____

_____

_____

_____

_____

Name _____ Date _____

Chapter 33 Test: Communism in Asia

A. **Sequencing. Number the events in the correct order using 1 for the event that happened first, 6 for the event that happened last, and so on.**

_____ The French moved back into Vietnam and reclaimed the southern part.

_____ Over ten thousand Vietnamese fought a guerilla war against the Japanese.

_____ The Japanese decreed that Vietnam would be ruled by a puppet emperor, Bao Dai.

_____ French and Vietnamese soldiers fought for eight years in the French Indochina War.

_____ Ho Chi Minh organized the Revolutionary Youth Organization and the Indochinese Communist Party.

_____ Ho Chi Minh announced that Vietnam was now a free country, called the Democratic Republic of Vietnam.

B. **Fill in the blanks.**

7. Ho Chi Minh gathered together all of the different revolutionary groups working secretly against the French and created a new rebel army called the _____.

8. The capital city of the Democratic Republic of Vietnam was _____.

9. _____ was the name of the French-controlled colony in the southern part of Vietnam.

10. The United States and the Soviet Union agreed to split Korea in half by drawing an imaginary line right at the _____.

11. When North Korean troops invaded South Korea, British and American soldiers under the command of _____ were sent to help.

12. _____ was the president of the United States when the Korean War began.

C. Short Answer. Answer each question using a complete sentence.

13. Why did Chiang Kai-shek throw Ho Chi Minh in jail for eighteen months?

_____

_____

_____

14. Why did Ho Chi Minh allow the French to put military bases in Vietnam?

_____

_____

_____

15. What happened to Vietnam at the end of the French Indochina War?

_____

_____

_____

16. How did the Soviet Union "help" Korea after World War II?

_____

_____

_____

17. Why did the Chinese get involved in the Korean War?

_____

_____

_____

18. What did the truce that ended the Korean War say?

_____

_____

_____

D. Essay. Answer the following question in paragraph form.

19. What problems did Korea face at the end of World War II?

_____

_____

_____

_____

_____

_____

The Story of the World

Chapter 34 Test: Dictators in South America and Africa

A. **Sequencing. Number the events in the correct order using 1 for the event that happened first, 6 for the event that happened last, and so on.**

_____ A group of military officers, including Juan Perón, went to Italy to study military strategies.

_____ Juan Perón was elected president of Argentina.

_____ The president of Argentina declared that the country would remain neutral during World War II.

_____ Juan Perón was arrested and put on a small island.

_____ Juan Perón fled Argentina and went first to Paraguay and then Spain.

_____ Military officers forced the president to resign and set up a military government.

B. **Fill in the blanks.**

7. In 1943, a group of military officers forced the president of Argentina to resign and then set up a military government, called a _____, to rule the country.

8. Juan Perón was a great admirer of _____ and how he ran the country of Italy.

9. The poor people of Argentina called Perón's wife _____, a nickname showing their love for her.

10. Patrice Lumumba organized a group called the _____, which led the movement for independence in the Congo.

11. When the eastern part of the Congo, known as the _____, declared itself independent, civil war broke out.

12. Today, the Congo is known by the African name _____.

C. Short Answer. Answer each question using a complete sentence.

13. Why were Argentinians divided about which side Argentina should join in World War II?

_____

_____

_____

14. What did Juan Perón do to become popular with the working poor of Argentina?

_____

_____

_____

15. How did Peron make sure that he kept his power?

_____

_____

_____

16. Why were many Africans upset that the Congo had become one big country called the Republic of the Congo?

_____

_____

_____

17. How did Mobutu gain power in the Congo?

_____

_____

_____

18. How did Mobutu keep his power in the Congo?

_____

_____

D. Essay. Answer the following question in paragraph form.

19. How did King Leopold II of Belgium mistreat the people of the Congo?

_____

_____

_____

_____

_____

_____

The Story of the World

Chapter 35 Test: The Cold War

A.   **Sequencing. Number the events in the correct order using 1 for the event that happened first, 6 for the event that happened last, and so on.**

_____ American spy planes, flying over Cuba, took pictures of nuclear weapons that had arrived in Cuba from the Soviet Union.

_____ Just after the beginning of World War II, Cubans voted on a new constitution that took away the United States' right to interfere in its affairs.

_____ Fidel Castro was arrested and thrown into prison for two years.

_____ The United States government planned an invasion of Cuba.

_____ General Batista led a military revolt and forced the Cuban president out of office.

_____ Castro and his allies took control of Cuba, and began to turn the country into a communist country.

B.   **Fill in the blanks.**

7.   In 1957, the Soviet Union launched a satellite, called _____, which was the first man-made satellite to ever be launched into space.

8.   After this satellite was launched, the United States created a new government agency, _____, to oversee the American space program.

9.   _____ was the first man to step on the moon's surface.

10.   After Fidel Castro gained power, many Cubans left Cuba and settled down in _____.

11.   _____ was the president of the United States when an invasion of Cuba was planned.

12.   Cubans, who had fled from Cuba to the United States, were trained by U.S. military officers, given American weapons, and then sent to invade Cuba, where they were supposed to land on a beach known as _____.

C. **Short Answer. Answer each question using a complete sentence.**

13. Why was the United States so worried when the Soviet Union launched its first satellite?

_____

_____

_____

14. What event made Americans determined to work even harder on their space program?

_____

_____

_____

15. What two things did the first astronauts leave on the moon? Why?

_____

_____

_____

16. What did Fidel Castro do when he gained control over the Cuban government?

_____

_____

_____

17. What are some of the reasons that thousands of Cubans left Cuba after Fidel Castro gained power?

_____

_____

_____

18. Why was the U.S. invasion of Cuba unsuccessful?

_____

_____

_____

D. Essay. Answer the following question in paragraph form.

19.   What was the Cuban Missile Crisis?

_____

_____

_____

_____

_____

_____

Name _____ Date _____

Chapter 36 Test: Struggles and Assassinations

A. **Sequencing. Number the events in the correct order using 1 for the event that happened first, 6 for the event that happened last, and so on.**

_____ The leader of the civil rights movement was assassinated in Memphis, Tennessee.

_____ The president sent federal troops to escort nine black students to school in Arkansas.

_____ Black southerners began to protest that segregation laws were unfair.

_____ Congress passed the Voting Rights Act, which guaranteed black people the right to vote.

_____ Rosa Parks refused to give up her seat on a bus in Montgomery, Alabama.

_____ Three lawyers brought a case before federal judges in Charleston, South Carolina, arguing that segregated schools violated the United States Constitution.

B. **Fill in the blanks.**

7.   President Kennedy was assassinated while visiting the city of _____.

8.   After President Kennedy died, people began to compare his presidency to _____, the mythical kingdom ruled by King Arthur.

9.   Most people believe that _____ was the man who shot Kennedy.

10. The segregation laws of the American South were nicknamed _____.

11. _____, the great civil rights leader, admired the ideas of Gandhi.

12. The _____ Act said that restaurants and other establishments could no longer discriminate on the basis of skin color.

C. Short Answer. Answer each question using a complete sentence.

13. What is one of the reasons that President Kennedy was so popular?

_____

_____

_____

14. Who became the new president after President Kennedy was shot?

_____

_____

_____

15. What happened to the man who was arrested for shooting President Kennedy?

_____

_____

_____

16. What did the Supreme Court decide in the case, Brown v. Board of Education?

_____

_____

_____

17. What did leaders of the civil rights movement do when Rosa Parks was arrested for refusing to give up her bus seat?

_____

_____

_____

18. Why did the president have to send federal troops to escort nine black students to school?

_____

_____

_____

D. Essay. Answer the following question in paragraph form.

19. How did America change after President Kennedy was assassinated?

_____

_____

_____

_____

_____

_____

The Story of the World

Chapter 37 Test: Two Short Wars and One Long One

A.   **Sequencing. Number the events in the correct order using 1 for the event that happened first, 6 for the event that happened last, and so on.**

_____ The president of Egypt was assassinated.

_____ Israel fought the Six-Day War against Syria, Egypt, and Jordan.

_____ The United States government announced that gas would be rationed.

_____ Peace talks were held in the United States between the president of Egypt and the prime minister of Israel.

_____ The Yom Kippur War began when Egypt and Syria attacked Israel.

_____ The president of Egypt, Anwar El-Sadat, wanted peace with Israel, and he spoke to the Israeli Parliament. He became the first Arab leader to ever visit Israel.

B.   **Fill in the blanks.**

7.   Members of Ho Chi Minh's revolutionary group were known in the southern part of Vietnam as the _____.

8.   President _____ began to pull U.S. troops out of Vietnam in 1969.

9.   The capital city of the southern part of Vietnam, _____, was renamed Ho Chi Minh City in 1975.

10. President _____ invited President Sadat of Egypt and the Prime Minister of Israel, Menachem Begin, to meet with him and discuss peace.

11. At the end of these peace talks, Sadat and Begin worked out an agreement known as the _____.

12. Sadat and Begin were awarded the _____ for their work at these peace talks.

C. Short Answer. Answer each question using a complete sentence.

13. What is a draft?

_____

_____

_____

14. What happened in Vietnam when the American soldiers left?

_____

_____

_____

15. How were American soldiers treated when they returned home from Vietnam?

_____

_____

_____

16. What was the result of the Six-Day War?

_____

_____

_____

17. Why did the president decide to send weapons to Israel during the Yom Kippur War?

_____

_____

_____

18. What caused the gas shortages in the United States?

_____

_____

_____

D. Essay. Answer the following question in paragraph form.

19. Why did the United States get involved in the Vietnam War?

_____

_____

_____

_____

_____

_____

Name _____ Date _____

Chapter 38 Test: Two Ways of Fighting

A. **Sequencing. Number the events in the correct order using 1 for the event that happened first, 6 for the event that happened last, and so on.**

_____ A rebel group killed the king of Afghanistan and announced that Afghanistan would be governed by ideas very much like communist ideas.

_____ The Soviet Union invaded Czechoslovakia.

_____ The Premier and Secretary of the Czech government were arrested and taken to Moscow.

_____ Civil war broke out in Afghanistan.

_____ Khrushchev was forced out of his position, and Leonid Brezhnev became the new premier of the Soviet Union.

_____ The Soviet Union invaded Afghanistan.

B. **Fill in the blanks.**

7. It was the job of the _____, the Russian Secret Police, to stamp out any opposition to the Soviet government.

8. When some Soviets managed to escape and get to Western Europe or the United States, they were known as _____.

9. Afghans who fought against the rebel government called themselves "righteous warriors" or _____.

10. The 1972 Summer Olympics were held in _____.

11. During the Olympics, terrorists broke into the rooms where the team from _____ slept. They killed two athletes and took nine more hostage.

12. These terrorists belonged to Black September, a group that had broken off from a larger terrorist group called the _____, or the PLO.

C. Short Answer. Answer each question using a complete sentence.

13. Why did people want to leave the Soviet Union?

_____

_____

_____

14. What problem did the Czechs have when the Soviets invaded?

_____

_____

_____

15. Why was Afghanistan not an easy country to conquer?

_____

_____

_____

16. What was the original goal of the PLO?

_____

_____

_____

17. What does a terrorist organization do when it "claims responsibility" for its attacks?

_____

_____

_____

18. Why did some members of the IRA split off and form the PIRA?

_____

_____

_____

D. **Essay. Answer the following question in paragraph form.**

19. How do terrorists fight?

_____

_____

_____

_____

_____

_____

The Story of the World

Chapter 39 Test: The 1980s in the East and the Mideast

A. **Sequencing. Number the events in the correct order using 1 for the event that happened first, 6 for the event that happened last, and so on.**

_____ West Pakistan dropped bombs on eight Indian airports.

_____ The Sikhs began to fight with Hindus—not just in the Punjab, but all through India.

_____ Mohandas Gandhi's friend and ally, Jawaharlal Nehru, became the prime minister of India.

_____ Nearly one thousand Sikh terrorists were killed when Indian soldiers stormed the Golden Temple in Amritsar.

_____ Indira Gandhi was assassinated.

_____ Indira Gandhi became India's prime minister.

B. **Fill in the blanks.**

7. Indira Gandhi convinced _____ to help India out with money and with exports of grain to feed the hungry in India.

8. East Pakistan changed its name to _____.

9. The Sikhs wanted to control their own part of India, an area called _____.

10. _____ was the last shah of Iran.

11. Ruhollah Khomeini was an _____, an Islamic religious leader.

12. When Khomeini became the leader of Iran, he turned Iran into a _____, a state ruled according to strict religious law.

C. **Short Answer. Answer each question using a complete sentence.**

13. Why did East Pakistan want to be free from West Pakistan?

_____

_____

_____

14. Why did the Sikhs decide to use the Golden Temple in Amritsar as their headquarters?

_____

_____

_____

15. What happened at the Union Carbide Corporation's factory in Bhopal?

_____

_____

_____

16. Why did Iran start to have trouble selling its oil?

_____

_____

_____

17. What happened during the Iranian Revolution?

_____

_____

_____

18. Why did Iran and Iraq fight an eight-year war?

_____

_____

_____

D. Essay. Answer the following question in paragraph form.

19. What happened during the White Revolution in Iran?

_____

_____

_____

_____

_____

_____

Name _____ Date _____

Chapter 40 Test: The 1980s in the USSR

A. **Sequencing. Number the events in the correct order using 1 for the event that happened first, 6 for the event that happened last, and so on.**

_____ For the first time, a town was powered entirely by nuclear power.

_____ The first commercial nuclear power plant opened.

_____ Scientists began to think about peaceful uses for nuclear power.

_____ A nuclear reactor exploded in Chernobyl, Russia.

_____ An accident at Three Mile Island frightened and angered the people nearby.

_____ Scientists managed to run a generator with nuclear power and produce enough electricity to light up four light bulbs.

B. **Fill in the blanks.**

7. In 1955, _____ became the first town to be powered entirely by nuclear power.

8. President _____ gave a speech to the United Nations called "Atoms for Peace" to assure people that nuclear power could be used for good.

9. Three Mile Island was a nuclear power plant in the state of _____.

10. Ronald Reagan, the American president who helped end the Cold War, had a strange nickname: _____.

11. _____, the leader of the Soviet Union, worked with Reagan to end the Cold War.

C. Short Answer. Answer each question using a complete sentence.

12. Why were scientists and government officials excited about nuclear power?

_____

_____

_____

13. Why did the accident at Three Mile Island frighten the people who lived nearby?

_____

_____

_____

14. What were the effects of the accident at Chernobyl?

_____

_____

_____

15. How did perestroika change the Soviet Union?

_____

_____

_____

16. What did glasnost mean to the people of the Soviet Union?

_____

_____

_____

17. What was the INF Treaty?

_____

_____

_____

D. Essay. Answer the following question in paragraph form.

18. What was Ronald Reagan's plan for ending the Cold War?

_____

_____

_____

_____

_____

_____

Name _____ Date _____

The Story of the World

Chapter 41 Test: Communism Crumbles—but Survives

A. **Sequencing. Number the events in the correct order using 1 for the event that happened first, 6 for the event that happened last, and so on.**

_____ East and West Germany were reunited into one country.

_____ East Germans began to hold large, loud protests and rallies.

_____ Ukraine, Lithuania, Latvia, and Armenia declared their independence from the USSR.

_____ The gates in the Berlin Wall were thrown open.

_____ A group of Berliners dug a 164-foot tunnel from a bakery in West Berlin to an outhouse in East Berlin.

_____ Eight communist conspirators surrounded Mikhail Gorbachev's house and ordered him to resign.

B. **Fill in the blanks.**

7. Chairman Mao thought that the best way for China to become the largest, most powerful, and wealthiest nation in the world was to copy _____.

8. Before Mao died, children were encouraged to join the _____, a youth military that swore loyalty to Mao.

9. Several years after Mao died, _____ became the leader of China.

10. The events that took place in Tiananmen Square were different from other similar events in the twentieth century because they happened on _____.

11. _____ thought that Gorbachev's reforms were happening too slowly and wanted to move towards a democracy much more quickly.

12. He became the leader of _____ after the breakup of the USSR.

C. Short Answer. Answer each question using a complete sentence.

13. What happened when the Chinese government forced farmers to combine their farms into collectives?

_____

_____

_____

14. What was the Cultural Revolution?

_____

_____

_____

15. After Mao died, what changes did the new leader of China make?

_____

_____

_____

16. What was life in East Germany like under communism?

_____

_____

_____

17. What happened to the Berlin Wall after the gates were finally opened?

_____

_____

_____

18. After the communist conspirators gave up, what did Gorbachev do?

_____

_____

_____

D. Essay. Answer the following question in paragraph form.

19. What happened in Tiananmen Square in 1989?

_____

_____

_____

_____

_____

_____

Name _____ Date _____

Chapter 42 Test: The End of the Twentieth Century

A. **Sequencing. Number the events in the correct order using 1 for the event that happened first, 6 for the event that happened last, and so on.**

_____ When the different countries of Africa began to ask for indepence, Ruanda-Urundi asked for independence from Belgium.

_____ The Tutsis invaded Rwanda and began to drive the Hutus out of the country.

_____ The Belgians divided Ruanda-Urundi into two separate countries, Rwanda in the north, and Burundi in the south.

_____ Tutsis who were driven from Rwanda formed a political party in exile, the Rwandan Patriotic Front.

_____ The Hutus put together a political party, held elections, and claimed the right to govern Ruanda-Urundi.

_____ The Hutu president of Rwanda was killed in a plane crash.

B. **Fill in the blanks.**

7. When Saddam Hussein invaded Kuwait, _____ immediately sent him a message telling him to withdraw his troops.

8. When he refused to leave, a group of soldiers from different nations began bombing factories and military bases in Iraq, starting with _____, the capital city.

9. The war to free Kuwait from Iraqi control was known as the _____ War.

10. _____ was an Anglican priest from South Africa who told the rest of the world about the evils of apartheid.

11. When P. W. Botha resigned, _____ became the new leader of South Africa.

12. _____ became the first black president of South Africa.

C. Short Answer. Answer each question using a complete sentence.

13. Why were other nations worried when Saddam Hussein invaded Kuwait?

_____

_____

_____

14. Who were some of the countries who helped free Kuwait from Iraqi control?

_____

_____

_____

15. What did Iraqi soldiers do as they retreated from Kuwait?

_____

_____

_____

16. What happened when the Tutsi invaded Rwanda and began to drive out the Hutus?

_____

_____

_____

17. What did the UN do to try to change things in South Africa?

_____

_____

_____

18. How did the rest of the world react to the unrest in South Africa?

_____

_____

_____

D. Essay. Answer the following question in paragraph form.

19. Why did Saddam Hussein invade Kuwait?

_____

_____

_____

_____

_____

_____

Answer Key

Chapter 1 Test

Sequencing: 5, 1, 6, 2, 4, 3

7. Crystal Palace   8. glass   9. Victoria   10. sepoys

11. Bahadur Shah   12. Viceroy

13. The people of London were afraid that if huge crowds walked inside the Crystal Palace and shook the ground with their feet, the whole building might collapse and kill everyone beneath.

14. The real reason for the Great Exhibition was to show the entire world how powerful and modern the British Empire was.

15. The British Empire included colonies in Canada, Australia, New Zealand, India, and South Africa. It was so large that the British said, "The sun never sets on the British Empire."

16. Indian soldiers did not want to serve on British ships because they would not be able to cook their own food and draw their own water for bathing, so they would be ceremonially unclean.

17. The last emperor of India, Bahadur Shah, was found guilty of treason by the British and sent away to live, under guard, in a distant city.

18. In an Enfield rifle, the bullets and powder were folded up together in a greased-paper package called a cartridge. The soldier would bite off the end of the cartridge and slide it into his rifle. Hindu soldiers worried that the grease used to coat the paper was made from the fat of cows, and cows are sacred to Hindus. Muslim soldiers worried that the grease was made from pig fat, and in Islam, pigs are unclean. Because the sepoys were already angry with their British superiors, they became convinced that the British were trying to destroy their Hindu and Muslim faith. The sepoys began to rebel all over the northwest of India.

Chapter 2 Test

Sequencing: 2, 4, 1, 5, 3, 6

7. Tokugawa   8. Matthew Perry   9. Millard Fillmore   10. Toda

11. Nicholas I   12. Sevastopol   13. Peace of Paris

14. In the mid-nineteenth century, the shogun had all of the power in Japan.

15. Japanese rulers were afraid that Christian missionaries would convert the Japanese to Christianity and destroy the Buddhist faith, and they were afraid that foreign armies would follow the missionaries and take over Japan.

16. American merchants wanted to buy fine silks and ceramics and coal from Japan.

17. The Russians wanted to capture Constantinople so that their ships could carry goods and soldiers down from the southern coast of Russia, through the Black Sea, past Constantinople, and into the Mediterranean Sea.

18. The French and the English suddenly became friends because they both wanted to stop the Russians from attacking the Turks and then moving on into Europe.

19. The countries involved in the Crimean War were ready to fight with each other for several reasons. The first reason was that while the Turks controlled the land of Palestine, they had given England, France, and several other Christian nations permission to take care of different holy places in Palestine. Another reason was that Nicholas I of Russia wanted to capture the city of Constantinople from the Turks so that he would have a way to sail into the Mediterranean Sea. A third reason was that England thought the Russians were wild and savage, and they were afraid that the Russians would try to take over Europe. A fourth reason was that France was also afraid of Russia, so the French decided to make friends with their long-time enemies, the English. All of these things meant that it didn't take much for these countries to begin fighting.

Chapter 3 Test

Sequencing: 2, 5, 3, 1, 6, 4

7. Kabul   8. Great Game   9. Scotland   10. Missionary Travels

11. Henry Stanley   12. Congo

13. Russia and Great Britain were interested in Afghanistan because it lay right between Russia and British-controlled India, and since Russia and Britain were enemies, neither country wanted the other to control the country between their two borders.

14. When the British offered to loan money to Dost Mohammad, he told the British government that Afghanistan would be a friend and ally as long as British soldiers would help him drive out the Indians who still lived in the southern parts of Afghanistan.

15. The British army was unpopular in Afghanistan because after British soldiers occupied the city of Kabul, they ate food that belonged to the Afghans, took whatever they wanted from the markets, and treated the people of Kabul with contempt.

16. David Livingstone's official job as consul was to find trade routes into Africa for British traders.

17. The *New York Times* sent one of its journalists to look for Livingstone because he spent so many years in the center of Africa that many people began to wonder whether or not he was still alive.

18. David Livingstone thought that if he explored Africa, he might find rivers and other trade routes that ran into the center of Africa. He hoped that if Europeans could reach the center of Africa easily, they could come in and trade with the Africans for ivory, salt, and other goods instead of slaves.

Chapter 4 Test

Sequencing: 2, 3, 1, 5, 6, 4

7. Young Italy   8. Giuseppe Garibaldi   9. Victor Emmanuel   10. Qing

11. opium   12. Taipings

13. Some of the secret societies wanted Italy to be a republic in which Italians would elect their own leaders and make their own laws, some wanted Italy to be ruled by the pope and the Catholic church, and still others wanted Italy to be ruled by a king.

14. The French king agreed to help the Italians fight against Austria because Victor Emmanuel promised to give the French king part of his own kingdom.

15. By the mid-nineteenth century, China had become poor because Chinese opium users gave British merchants huge amounts of money for opium, but the British didn't spend nearly as much of their money on Chinese goods. So more money was leaving China than was coming into it.

16. Hong Xiuquan believed that his dream was a message from God calling him to fight against the evils that made the poor people of China miserable.

17. Hong Xiuquan's followers grew their hair long to show that they were enemies of the Qing.

18. The British helped the Qing fight against the revolutionaries because China had signed a treaty that would open up more Chinese ports to British merchants as soon as the rebellion was put down.

19. The Taipings planned to divide Chinese land up evenly, with men and women getting equal shares. Families would grow crops and keep as much as they needed for themselves while putting the rest into a public store. All men and women would be brothers and sisters. One Taiping leader even suggested that China hold elections for it leaders, like Western countries.

Chapter 5 Test

Sequencing: 3, 6, 4, 1, 5, 2

7. Robert E. Lee   8. Ulysses S. Grant   9. Emancipation Proclamation

10. Richmond, Va. or Atlanta, Ga.   11. John Wilkes Booth   12. Reconstruction

13. Farmers in the south needed cheap labor to work in their tobacco and cotton fields.

14. The northern states did not have huge fields of crops that needed tending; they had factories, mills, and ironworks instead.

15. The southern states wanted slavery to be legal in the new states, so that the northern states would be outnumbered. The northern states wanted slavery to be illegal in the new states, so that slave-holding states wouldn't overwhelm the rest of the U.S.

16. President Lincoln's assassination showed how much hatred still remained in the country.

17. The Thirteenth Amendment to the Constitution made slavery illegal in every state in the union.

18. After the Civil War, the United States still faced problems. In the South, hundreds of towns and cities had been burned and destroyed. Over five hundred thousand men had been killed, and in the South, a whole generation had been wiped out. Although slaves had been freed, the government did not help the former slaves to get any land where they could live. They did not win any payment for the years they had spent working for their masters. They had to try to earn their own living, usually on farms owned by white farmers who were bitter that the United States had taken away their slaves. The free blacks were often treated just as badly as they had been during slavery.

Chapter 6 Test

Sequencing: 6, 4, 5, 2, 1, 3

7. creoles   8. Argentina   9. War of the Triple Alliance

10. Ontario   11. Quebec   12. Nova Scotia

13. López planned to get control of the rivers that led into Argentina and Brazil so that he could sail down and attack these countries.

14. The soldiers of Brazil, Argentina, and Uruguay used the new Enfield rifles while the Paraguayan soldiers only had old-fashioned flintlock muskets, which didn't always fire.

15. Some Paraguayans think López was a patriot who fought for the freedom of his country against the schemes of Argentina and Brazil. Others think he was an insane dictator.

16. Papineau encouraged the people of Canada to protest the power of the English governor.

17. The Earl of Durham suggested the Assemblies be given the power to govern their own country so that the Canadian provinces would never rebel again.

18. The British North American Act formed the provinces of Quebec, Ontario, Nova Scotia, and New Brunswick into a new country called the Dominion of Canada. It also explained how the western territories of Canada could be formed into provinces, and then drawn into the Dominion of Canada.

19. Many Canadians were afraid that the western territories of Canada would be taken by the United States, unless Canadians could join together and claim those territories for a strong, united Canada. However, smaller provinces, like Prince Edward Island, were afraid that a federation would give the larger provinces too much power. So the provinces argued and argued about forming a federation until four provinces joined together and agreed to pass the British North American Act.

Chapter 7 Test

Sequencing: 2, 3, 4, 1, 6, 5

7. Bourbon   8. Lafayette   9. Napoleon   10. Austria

11. Second Reich   12. Wilhelm II

13. In a constitutional monarchy, a country has a king, but the king must obey a written set of laws, instead of doing whatever he pleases.

14. Louis-Napoleon took power away from the assembly because they wouldn't give him all the money he wanted, and they wouldn't agree to let him run for president a second time.

15. The second French Empire ended when the Prussians captured Napoleon III.

16. In a confederacy, states agree together to elect officials who will be in charge of dealing with foreign countries and other matters that affect all of the states, but each state stays independent, with its own government and its own identity.

17. Otto von Bismarck earned the nickname of the "Iron Chancellor" when he announced that Prussia would become the strongest of the German states not "by speeches and majority votes, but by blood and iron."

18. The German states would not allow Wilhelm to call himself the Emperor of Germany because none of the German states wanted to belong to a country called "Germany."

19. Friedrich was disturbed by Prussia's overwhelming influence on the German states because he felt that Bismarck had made Prussia great and powerful by making them conquerors and destroyers. He thought that the rest of the world did not love or respect the Prussians, but only feared them. He wrote that Bismarck had robbed the Prussians of their friends, the sympathies of the world, and their conscience.

Chapter 8 Test

Sequencing: 2, 4, 1, 5, 3, 6

7. Thomas Edison   8. sun   9. Sir Sandford Fleming   10. Tokyo

11. Satsuma Revolt   12. Meiji Restoration

13. Before the railroad was built, a business man who wanted to travel across the United States would have take a month-long journey by stagecoach, or sail in a steamship all the way around the coast of South America.

14. The railroad across the United States was completed at Promontory Summit, Utah, on May 10, 1869.

15. When time became standardized, it was kept according to the same rules across the whole United States, and eventually, across the whole world.

16. Yoshinobu agreed to resign as shogun because he knew that a civil war would weaken Japan and make her even less able to stand up to the United States and other countries of the West.

17. The conscripts in the new Japanese army were supposed to fight in return for a salary, not like the samurai who fought because they owed a feudal obligation to a nobleman.

18. Under Japan's new constitution, a group of advisors to the emperor, known as the cabinet, made the policies for the country.

19. Railroads changed the United States by carrying people to cities where they might never have settled and allowing companies to make large amounts of money from shipping grain, cattle, coal, and other goods to far-away places of the United States. Time zones meant that people could now set their clocks according to time zones, not according to the sun. Light bulbs meant that dusk was no longer the end of the working day. Men could go on laboring, long after sunset.

Chapter 9 Test

Sequencing: 4, 1, 6, 3, 2, 5

7. Sumatra

8. guerrilla

9. Ibu Perbu or The Queen

10. sultan

11. Balkans

12. Bulgaria

13. Merchants from the Netherlands formed the Dutch East India Company and built trading posts on the islands east of India. They called these islands the East Indies, and then the Dutch East Indies when the Dutch government took over control of the ports.

14. The kingdom of Acheh was allowed to remain independent so that it would be a neutral zone between the British in Singapore and the Dutch in Sumatra.

15. Farmers in the East Indies began to revolt because the Dutch government forced them to set apart one fifth of their land to grow crops for the Dutch and spend three days a week working on this land, rather than on their own.

16. Abdul Aziz ordered his soldiers to kill all of the Bulgarian revolutionaries and anyone who had helped them. His soldiers wiped out sixty villages and killed almost twelve thousand Bulgarians.

17. Abdulhamid II announced that the Ottoman Empire would have a constitution, like the modern Western countries, and an assembly that would meet together to make laws.

18. The Russians said that when the Turkish army had wiped out Bulgarian villages, Muslim soldiers had killed many Bulgarian Christians, and that the Christians of Russia were obliged to help protect their fellow believers.

19. The Ottoman Empire was known as the "sick man of Europe" because for many years, the Ottoman Turks had been growing weaker and poorer. The sultans spent so much money that they had to borrow money from other countries just to pay the soldiers in the Turkish army. In addition, people in three parts of the Ottoman Empire, the Balkans, Anatolia, and Lebanon, were starting to ignore the sultan.

Chapter 10 Test

Sequencing: 3, 1, 5, 4, 2, 6

7. Andes

8. War of the Pacific

9. Huáscar

10. Suez

11. khedive

12. Ottoman

13. Peru helped Bolivia in the war against Chile because the two countries had signed a treaty six years earlier promising to always be each other's allies—especially against Chile.

14. As a result of the War of the Pacific, Bolivia had to give up its entire coastline and became "landlocked."

15. After the War of the Pacific, the people of Peru were so angry and unhappy that civil war broke out and went on for seven years.

16. Muhammad Ali tried to make Egypt more like the countries of Europe by bringing university professors from Europe into Egypt, to teach Egyptian students about the West.

17. The countries of Europe were interested in the new canal because they could use it to travel to the Far East to trade. It would shorten the trip from Europe to the East by six thousand miles.

18. Ismail Pasha spent too much money on his projects and had to start borrowing money from France and Great Britain.

19. The Atacama Desert lies in a "rain shadow" so it is the driest place in the whole world. The ground is made of salt, sand, and hardened lava. The soil is as barren and lifeless as the soil on Mars. Bolivia and Chile both wanted to control the Atacama Desert because of the chemicals and minerals that lie in it. Copper, saltpeter, used to make gunpowder, and sodium nitrate, used to make fertilizer and bombs, are all found in the Atacama Desert.

Chapter 11 Test

Sequencing: 5, 3, 2, 6, 4, 1

7. bushrangers   8. Melbourne   9. Belgium

10. Germany   11. The Scramble   12. Liberia, Ethiopia

13. Ned Kelly believed that poor farmers could never be treated fairly by the police, and that the government would always be on the side of the rich.

14. Some Australians thought that Ned Kelly was just a common criminal, but others thought that he was a hero, fighting against cruel and unjust police and government officials.

15. When Australia became the Commonwealth of Australia, it meant that Australia would remain part of the British Empire, but the Australians would have the right to make their own laws and elect their own leaders.

16. The countries of Europe were interested in Africa because Africa was filled with gold, silver, limestone, rubber plants, and wide fields that were perfect for cotton, coffee, and tea.

17. The International African Association was a "charity" created by Leopold II as a way to claim the land in the Congo Basin.

18. The purpose of the Berlin Conference was to divide all of the African land fairly among the countries of Europe.

19. The Berlin Conference was supposed to prevent war by fairly dividing the land of Africa among the European nations, but it caused years of unrest in Africa. When the countries of Europe began to draw lines around new colonies, they often drew their lines so that they divided friendly African tribes from each other and locked hostile tribes together inside the same country borders. The countries of Europe took power away from the African tribal chiefs and leaders and ignored the customs and traditions of these tribes who had lived in Africa for thousands of years.

Chapter 12 Test

Sequencing: 5, 3, 2, 6, 1, 4

7. potatoes   8. Robert Peel   9. William Gladstone

10. gold   11. Boer   12. Mafeking

13. Most of the Irish were Catholic, and the Protestant kings and queens of England did not treat the Irish very well.

14. The Corn Laws said that anyone in Ireland or England who bought food from another country had to pay a huge tax on it.

15. The Home Rule Bill would have allowed the Irish to have control over issues that had to do with life in Ireland and did not affect the British.

16. The Boers began to call themselves Afrikaners to show that they were no longer Dutch settlers, but rather Africans of European descent.

17. The Afrikaners declared war on Great Britain because they could see that the British intended to take over Transvaal and the Free State.

18. The Peace of Vereeniging united all of the South African colonies into one nation under British rule. Inside this country lived three groups that hated each other—white British, white Afrikaners, and black Africans.

19. The blight was a disease that killed all of the potatoes in Ireland for five years. Because many of the Irish lived on farms that were owned by British landlords, most of the crops that they grew were shipped off to England to be sold. Only the potatoes remained in Ireland. When the potato crop died, the people of Ireland had nothing to eat. Almost one million Irish people died during these five years, and another million left their homes and went to other countries. And because the British government did nothing to help the Irish during the famine, Irish hatred of English rule grew even stronger.

Chapter 13 Test

Sequencing: 2, 1, 4, 3, 5, 6

7. Portugal   8. slavery   9. republic

10. Red   11. Turkey   12. Young Turks

13. The five groups of people who lived in Brazil during the reign of Pedro II were the descendants of Portuguese settlers, South American Indian tribes, African slaves, European immigrants, and American cotton planters.

14. The Council of State told Pedro II that he should leave Brazil because they thought it was time for Brazil to become a republic without an old-fashioned emperor.

15. Today, Brazilians think of Pedro II has a hero who spent years serving his country.

16. Article 113 of the Turkish constitution said that the sultan could deport anyone he thought "harmful to the state."

17. The Armenians were not treated well in the Ottoman Empire because the Armenians were Christians, and the Ottomans were Muslim.

18. The students at Istanbul University wanted their country to be ruled by secular laws rather than a country ruled by an Islamic sultan.

19. Pedro II encouraged Brazilian companies to build modern factories and railroads. He started new schools so that all groups of people would have the opportunity to get an education, work, and earn a good living. He begged skilled workers from other countries to come and settle in Brazil. He traveled to other European countries to see their scientific inventions and their factories. Most importantly, he got rid of slavery.

Chapter 14 Test

Sequencing: 4, 2, 3, 1, 6, 5

7. Romanov   8. Siberia   9. Nicholas II

10. Liberia   11. King of Kings   12. Lion of Africa

13. As soon as Alexander III became czar, he began to take away all of the new freedoms that his father had given to the Russian people.

14. Alexander II tried to make Russia more Western by building railroads and new schools. He gave newspaper editors and writers more freedom to say whatever they wanted. He gave the towns of Russia permission to govern themselves. He decreed that anyone accused of a crime had the right to be tried by a jury, rather than being sentenced by a judge, so that powerful, corrupt judges could not convict innocent men unjustly.

15. Life for the Jews of Russia was even worse than other poor Russians because they had to pay more taxes, were forced to live in certain areas of Russia, and weren't allowed to move wherever they pleased.

16. Italy tricked Menelik into signing a treaty that made Ethiopia a protectorate of Italy. The treaty said one thing in Menelik's language, and another thing in Italian.

17. The Italians were outnumbered at the Battle of Adowa by more than five to one. They had such bad maps that they didn't know where to hide, and a huge rainstorm poured down and confused them even more.

18. Italy, Great Britain, and France all signed treaties recognizing Ethiopia's independence because none of them wanted the others to gain any more power in Africa, so if one tried to invade Ethiopia, the other two would stop it.

19. Alexander III cancelled Alexander II's decree that the towns could govern themselves. He allowed the Russian noblemen to oppress the poor peasants who worked on their land. Anyone who opposed him or criticized him was sent away to Siberia.

Chapter 15 Test

Sequencing: 1, 4, 5, 2, 6, 3

7. Queen Min   8. Korea   9. sugarcane

10. William Randolph Hearst, Joseph Pulitzer   11. Theodore Roosevelt   12. Rough Riders

13. Korea became known as the Hermit Country because it would only trade with China and send ambassadors only to China.

14. At the end of the Sino-Japanese War, China signed a treaty that gave Korea total independence and gave the Japanese large territories once held by China. Many European countries also took advantage of China's weakness to seize other bits of China for themselves.

15. When Queen Min asked the Russians to become Korea's ally, she was assassinated.

16. The hidden message in José Rizal's novel, Touch Me Not, was that the Spanish government was cruel, unjust, and oppressive.

17. American newspapers were eager for the United States to declare war on Spain because during war, hundreds of thousands of people bought newspapers to find out what was happening.

18. The Treaty of Paris decreed that Puerto Rico, Cuba, the Philippines, and Guam would be ruled by the United States instead of Spain.

19. China and Japan had made an agreement with each other about Korea. Since neither country wanted the other to take control of Korea, they agreed that Korea would be protected by both of them, and that neither of them could send soldiers into Korea without the agreement of the other country. When King Kojong asked China for help to put down the Tonghak Rebellion, China sent a warship loaded with soldiers to Korea. Japan was angry that China had broken their agreement, so the Japanese sank the warship with all of the Chinese soldiers on board. Then China and Japan declared war on each other.

Chapter 16 Test

Sequencing: 4, 2, 1, 3, 5, 6

7. reservations   8. Crazy Horse   9. Geronimo   10. stockholder

11. corporation   12. philanthropist

13. Many Americans decided to move west because it was getting hard for workers to find jobs in the cities, and it was getting hard for farmers to find land to buy.

14. A western territory could become a state when sixty thousand people had settled there.

15. At the Battle of Little Bighorn, General George Custer and hundreds of his men were killed by almost four thousand Native American warriors led by Crazy Horse.

16. People had to stop selling the goods that they made in their homes because the factories could make the same goods cheaper and quicker and therefore sell them for less.

17. The home workers were forced to go work in the factories.

18. Andrew Carnegie gave away 350 million dollars for college scholarships, libraries, scientific research, and many other good causes.

19. Andrew Carnegie believed that the poor had less wisdom and ability than the rich. He thought that an average man who got rich would just squander his money, but a man who was smart enough to earn enormous wealth was also smart enough to use that money for the good of mankind. He thought it was better for the country to have some people that were poor because they didn't have the ability to spend money wisely anyway. Then the very rich would spend money on their behalf.

Chapter 17 Test

Sequencing: 5, 3, 2, 4, 6, 1

7. Cixi, the Empress Dowager   8.   Forbidden City   9. embassies

10. Korea   11. Admiral Togo   12. Theodore Roosevelt

13. Guangxu made himself unpopular by changing China's government, law, schools, money systems, army, and police so that China would be more modern.

14. The Boxers pulled up railway lines in China because almost all of the railroads in China had been built by European merchants, with European money, in order to bring trains filled with European soldiers, European goods, and European customs into the center of China.

15. The result of the Boxer Rebellion was that Western countries had managed to take control of Chinese affairs.

16. Port Arthur was important because it was Russia's only good port that lay on the Pacific, and without it, Russia had no way to move troops and supplies by sea.

17. The Russians were confident that Japan would not attack them, because Russia had the third largest navy in the world, and the new modern Japanese army had not been in existence for very long.

18. The war between Russia and Japan showed the world that Japan was now the master of the East.

19. The Boxers were a group of Chinese men and women who were fiercely patriotic, but who didn't think that their government was doing a very good job protecting the Chinese people. They wanted to get rid of all Western people and Western ideas in China. They planned on doing this by attacking missionaries from the West and Chinese Christians. They thought that Chinese Christians were traitors to their country and that missionaries had brought Western ways into China and destroyed the traditions of the Chinese. The Boxers also wanted to get rid of all of the railroads that the Westerners had built.

Chapter 18 Test

Sequencing: 5 , 1, 6, 3, 4, 2

7. Tehran   8.   Majles   9. Balkan

10. St. Elijah's Day   11. Islamic   12. Austria

13. Mozaffar od-Din Shah sold permission to develop an oil field to William Knox D'Arcy.

14. Great Britain and Russia had power over Persia because Persia owed both of the countries huge amounts of money.

15. Mohammad Ali Shah thought that taking stronger control over his own country might help him deal with Great Britain and Russia, so he dissolved the Majles. The Persian people were so angry that they drove the shah out of the country.

16. When Abdulhamid ordered his soldiers to march into Macedonia and kill the rebels, the violence disgusted many Ottoman Turks.

17. The Young Turks' Proclamation for the Ottoman Empire said that the government would do what the people wanted.

18. Most of the people of Macedonia and Albania were Christians, so they did not want to be a part of an Ottoman nation where most of the people were Muslim.

19. The British were interested in Persia because they wanted to keep Russia's power from growing, and they needed oil. Most of Great Britain's ships were coal-burning ships, which required many sailors to spend their time shoveling coal. Oil-burning ships needed only a few men to run the engines so the rest of the men could be manning guns. Oil-burning ships ran faster and had to refuel less often. The British discovered that the Germans were building oil-burning ships, and they did not want the German navy to be stronger and faster than the British navy. So the British wanted to build more oil-burning ships, and Persia would be a good reliable source of oil to power those new ships.

Chapter 19 Test

Sequencing: 3, 1, 4, 2, 6, 5

7. Henry Puyi   8. Nationalist Party   9. Nanjing

10. Indochina   11. Nguyen   12. Tonkin, Annam, Cochin China

13. During the reign of Puyi, Russia, Japan, and the United States controlled China.

14. The people of the Sichuan Province were trying to build their own railroad, and they revolted when the Chinese government tried to take over the project.

15. The last emperor of China, Henry Puyi, was forced to abdicate.

16. The Vietnamese were unhappy with the French because the French made most of the money in Vietnam, and Vietnamese citizens were not allowed to hold important jobs.

17. Phan Boi Chau was living in China when he tried to organize rebellions against the French, and it was hard to start a revolt while living in another country.

18. Today the Vietnamese consider Phan Boi Chau one of the greatest Vietnamese patriots.

19. Sun Yixian's Three Principles of the People were the rules by which he wanted the people of China to live, rather than following the rule of an emperor. The First Principle was democracy. The Chinese should be able to vote for their leaders. The Second Principle was livelihood. Everyone in China should be able to find a job and earn enough to buy food. The Third Principle was nationalism. The Chinese, not foreigners, should run the country of China.

Chapter 20 Test

Sequencing: 4, 3, 1, 6, 2, 5

7. Pancho Villa   8. Victoriano Huerta   9. The Great War

10. Central Powers   11. Allied Forces   12. draft

13. Porfirio Díaz was the president of Mexico for so long because whenever someone else tried to run against him, Díaz's supporters scared the opponent away.

14. When Francisco Madero ran against Díaz, Díaz had Madero arrested and thrown into jail, and then Díaz's officials announced that Mexicans had once again elected Díaz president.

15. During the Ten Tragic Days, Madero's troops and rebel fighters shot at each other inside Mexico City. The shells set off fires and burned homes and stores throughout the city.

16. When Germany ignored Belgium's declaration of neutrality, the British worried that Germany would take over all of Europe.

17. The rest of the world was furious when the Germans sank the *Lusitania* because the *Lusitania* was a passenger ship filled with civilians. Sinking it broke all the rules of war.

18. The United States entered World War I when the Germans sent a secret telegram promising to return to Mexico land that America had claimed during the Mexican War if Mexico would fight on the side of the Germans.

19. When Francisco Madero finally became president of Mexico, all of the rebel leaders who had helped fight for Díaz's removal had different ideas about how Mexico should be reformed. Some of them just wanted free elections. Others wanted the government to take the land owned by foreign businessmen way from them, and give it back to the people. The rich men of Mexico, even those who had supported Madero's presidency, wanted as little change as possible.

Chapter 21 Test

Sequencing: 3, 6, 2, 5, 4, 1

7. Rasputin   8. Aleksandr Kerensky   9. Communist Party

10. Woodrow Wilson   11. doughboys   12. suffragettes

13. The Russian army was not well prepared. Almost two million Russian soldiers marched into battle with no weapons at all.

14. Lenin thought the peasants had the right to take over land owned by the wealthy because the wealthy had often earned their money by forcing the poor to work hard for very little reward.

15. The Bolsheviks believed that Christianity was false and wrong, so they changed the names of the cities in Russia that were named after Christian saints.

16. President Wilson thought that the United States had to join the war so that the democratic countries of Europe would not lose their right to elect their own leaders.

17. During World War I, American women did the jobs that men left behind when they went off to war. They also joined the Navy and Marine Corps and served as nurses, clerks, telephone operators, electricians, and photographers.

18. Since women had done the men's jobs perfectly well during World War I, it seemed obvious that women should be allowed to vote.

19. Lenin tackled the problem of Russian poverty in a new way. He wanted to make sure that the wealthy didn't own all the land while the poor had none. So the Communist Party decided that all of the land in the country would belong to the government, and the government would allow people to use the land equally. Instead of individual Russians building businesses, making money, and perhaps forcing other Russians to work for little pay, the government would own and run most of the businesses. This new way of living, called communism, was supposed to make sure that the government, instead of a small group of powerful people, had control over Russia. But the government was controlled by a small group of people, Lenin and his followers.

Chapter 22 Test

Sequencing: 1, 5, 2, 3, 6, 4

7. Gaelic   8. Ulster   9. Irish Republican Army

10. Raj   11. Delhi   12. Congress Party

13. Many of the people who lived in northern Ireland were Protestants, and they were worried that if Irish self-rule were restored, they might be treated badly by the Catholic majority.

14. During the Easter Uprising, Irish rebels took control of the post office and government buildings in Dublin. British troops marched in to put down the rebellion, and after a week of fighting almost four hundred people had been killed.

15. The treaty between Sinn Féin and the British government said that most of Ireland would become a country called the Irish Free State, which would rule itself with its own parliament but would remain loyal to the British monarch. Ulster, however, would remain part of Great Britain.

16. The British tried to improve life in India by building roads and railroads, laying telegraph lines, and improving India's harbors so that more ships could trade in Indian ports.

17. When demonstrators met in Amritsar to protest against British rule, British soldiers fired at the unarmed demonstrators without any warning. Over three hundred people died and over a thousand were wounded.

18. Satyagraha is the nonviolent fight for freedom and justice.

19. Gandhi encouraged his followers to resist British rule by refusing to pay taxes to the British government and boycotting British goods. He told his followers to make their own handmade cloth for their clothes instead of buying British cotton. When the British put a tax on salt, Gandhi led his followers on a 240-mile march to go collect salt from the sea. He told Indians to take their children out of British schools, and asked them to give up privileges given to them by the British. He went on a hunger strike when a factory refused to give its workers enough money to live on.

Chapter 23 Test

Sequencing: 3, 2, 5, 4, 1, 6

7. Versailles

8. Yugoslavia

9. Czechoslovakia

10. White, Red

11. Leningrad

12. Siberia

13. The League of Nations was an organization formed by the Versailles Peace Settlement. Countries that had an argument would bring their problem to the League of Nations, and countries in the League would decide what should be done to settle the argument.

14. Article 231 said that Germany was solely responsible for the war and had to pay over thirty-two billion dollars in losses and damages to other countries.

15. The new countries created by the peace settlement had boundaries drawn by people who didn't live in them. These boundaries forced people who had different cultures and histories and who sometimes hated each other to become citizens of the same countries.

16. A totalitarian state is a country with only one political party, and no one gets to disagree with the way that party runs the country.

17. Joseph Stalin planned to make Russia great by building factories and mines. He wanted steelworks that would make new rails for railroads, and parts for electrical generators that would light up Russia's homes and streets.

18. On collective farms, hundreds of farmers worked in the same fields, and almost all of the food grown in these fields went into a "common stockpile" controlled by the government.

19. The three most powerful leaders at the conference in Versailles were Woodrow Wilson, the president of the United States, David Lloyd George, the prime minister of Great Britain, and Georges Clemenceau, the French prime minister. Wilson thought the most important job of the conference was to figure out how to keep such a war from happening again. He wanted all of the countries of the world to join the League of Nations. Lloyd George was worried that Russia might decide to spread communism through force, by conquering other countries in Europe. He wanted to make sure that the Germans did not feel so desperate that they were willing to become a communist country and form an alliance with Russia. Clemenceau had seen much of his country destroyed, so he simply wanted Germany to be punished.

Chapter 24 Test

Sequencing: 3, 1, 5, 4, 6, 2

7. sultan

8. Wafd

9. King Fu'ad I

10. Adriatic Sea

11. Fascists

12. Il Duce

13. Egypt was important to Great Britain because the Suez Canal made the trip from Britain to Japan six thousand miles shorter.

14. After Britain granted Egypt is freedom, Egypt became a constitutional monarchy with a king whose powers were limited by a constitution and by an elected assembly.

15. The Wafd, the king, and the British were all involved in a three-way struggle for power.

16. Mussolini thought the most important thing for any country was that its government be strong.

17. The Italians were poor, unhappy, and had no leader at all, so the idea that a strong leader might take control, fix all of Italy's problems, and return Italy to a glorious place as the strongest nation in Europe was wonderful.

18. Mussolini's ultimate goal for Italy was to build a new Roman Empire by recapturing land all around the Mediterranean Sea.

19. Italy's prime minister was not allowed to help write the treaty that ended World War I because Great Britain and France didn't trust him. Before the war, Italy had made an alliance with Germany and Austria. Although Italy broke that alliance when the war began, the Italians did not immediately help the Allies. Instead, Italy stayed out of the war for a year while thousands of French and British soldiers died. So after the war, Italy was still treated with suspicion, because Italy had once been Germany's friend and hadn't immediately joined with Germany's enemies.

Chapter 25 Test

Sequencing: 1, 4, 3, 6, 2, 5

7. Nationalist Party   8. Manchukuo   9. Henry Puyi

10. manifesto   11. Mao Zedong   12. Chinese Soviet Republic or Kiangsi Soviet

13. When Yuan Shikai took over the Chinese government, he had to fight off other warlords to keep his power.

14. Sun Yixian and Chiang Kai-shek asked Russia to send help so that the Nationalist Party could fight against the warlords and unite China into a republic.

15. Hirohito didn't order the Japanese army to leave Manchuria because if the army refused to go, then it would be obvious to everyone that the Japanese assembly and the emperor were helpless.

16. Many Chinese thought that the Soviet Union was a good model for a new China because they had seen the devastation caused by the weakness of the Qing emperor, and the struggle for power between warlords that followed.

17. Chiang Kai-shek thought that the Russians had too much power in the Chinese Communist Party, and he agreed with others who accused the CCP of helping foreigners to once again gain control over China.

18. The Long March was the one-year journey that Mao and his follower took from the Kiangsi Soviet to the town of Wuqi when they were fleeing the National Revolutionary Army.

19. Chiang Kai-shek was forced to make peace with the Chinese Communist Party because many people were beginning to wonder why he was spending so much energy fighting the CCP, when the Japanese were trying to take away more and more of Manchuria. These people thought the Nationalist Army should be fighting against the Japanese instead of fighting other Chinese. The CCP began to use their slogan, "Chinese don't fight Chinese." Many people agreed with this slogan, including soldiers in the Nationalist Army who didn't want to fight against the CCP any more. When Chiang Kai-shek was held prisoner by a commanding officer of the Nationalist Army, he realized that he would only make his authority weaker by continuing to fight. It was time for him to make peace with the CCP.

Chapter 26 Test

Sequencing: 2, 3, 5, 6, 1, 4

7. Wall Street   8. Great Depression   9. Dust Bowl   10. reparations   11. Nazis   12. Jews

13. The stock market is a place where people buy stock, a small portion of a company.

14. The Reconstruction Finance Corporation was a bank that was set up by President Hoover and Congress that would lend money to banks, businesses, and farms, so that they could keep going until times got a little better.

15. Franklin Roosevelt created new "companies," such as the Civilian Conservation Corps, The Works Progress Administration, and the Agricultural Adjustment Administration, that would give Americans jobs and salaries.

16. Hitler thought that Germany was the strongest, worthiest country in the world, and that German culture was the most beautiful. He wanted to spread German ways all across Europe.

17. Europeans had been suspicious of Jews since the Middle Ages. They knew almost nothing about Jewish culture and the Jewish religion, and they thought the Jews were proud, boastful, and cared about nothing but money.

18. The Germans were willing to listen to Hitler because they were already poor and discouraged. When the Great Depression hit, they were poorer, hungrier, and more desperate, and they were willing to listen to anyone who could promise them a better future.

19. After the end of World War I, factories and companies were making huge amounts of money. People who bought stock in those companies were making lots of money, too. Buying stock seemed like the easiest way in the world to earn money. People were so excited about buying stock, that sometimes they even borrowed money to buy stock. Then more factories were built and more companies were started. As more businesses were built, there were not as many buyers to go around. In late October of 1929, people started to sell off their stock. Then other people began to think that they should sell their stock, too. There were so many people selling their stock, and not many people wanted to buy any stock, so the prices of the stocks kept going down and down. This caused even more people to sell their stock, because they wanted to get some money back before the prices dropped even more. This selling went on for a week and became known as the Wall Street Crash.

Chapter 27 Test

Sequencing: 4, 3, 6, 2, 5, 1

7. Red Spain   8. Black Spain   9. Catalonia

10. Austria   11. Sudetenland   12. Axis Powers, Allied Powers

13. When Spain sent its army to stop a revolt in Morocco, over ten thousand Spanish soldiers were killed by the much smaller army of Moroccan rebels.

14. During the Spanish Civil War, the Nationalists, who wanted a strong, decisive leader like Mussolini of Italy, fought against the Popular Front, the Spaniards who wanted Spain to keep its constitution.

15. When Francisco Franco gained power over the whole country, he ruled as a military dictator and used his army to control the country.

16. France and Great Britain were more afraid of communism than they were of Germany, and they did not want to have another war like the Great War. They thought that if Hitler had a large army, then the Soviet Union wouldn't be able to claim Germany as a communist country.

17. Hitler made a deal with Joseph Stalin that if the Soviets would help Germany conquer Poland, Germany and Russia would divide Poland between them.

18. When Germany invaded Poland, France and Great Britain realized that there would be no peace, and they finally declared war on Hitler.

19. Hitler planned to claim Europe for Germany a little bit at a time. First he wanted to reunite Germany by taking over all of the countries where German-speaking people lived. He said that he would be recreating the "Fatherland" that had existed in older times and had been destroyed. So first he claimed Austria for Germany, and then he added Czechoslovakia. He also made an alliance with Italy, so Mussolini's soldiers would support Hitler's army. When Hitler moved into Poland, France and Great Britain finally declared war.

Chapter 28 Test

Sequencing: 4, 6, 2, 5, 1, 3

7. Franklin Roosevelt   8. Hirohito   9. Midway

10. Aryans   11. Jesse Owens   12. Denmark

13. By declaring itself an Axis power, Japan gave itself the perfect excuse to attack the colonies held by the Allies in southeast Asia, such as Hong Kong, Vietnam, and the East Indies.

14. Before the Japanese attacked, the United States had agreed to send oil, guns, and other necessary supplies to Great Britain, but that was as far as most Americans wanted to go.

15. Japan attacked the U.S. fleet at Pearl Harbor because they knew that the United States was the one country standing in the way of its conquest of Asia.

16. In every territory claimed by Germany, Jews were forced to wear yellow six-pointed stars known as the "Star of David."

17. Kristallnacht was a night when all over Germany, German mobs broke windows and burned many of the houses and shops owned by Jews.

18. In France, clergymen helped Jewish children hide and escape to Switzerland. Dutch families like the ten Booms hid Jews in their basements and helped them escape. In Poland, the director of the Warsaw Zoo hid Jewish children in the cages, beneath the straw, so that Nazi soldiers couldn't find them.

19. Hitler's "final solution" for the "problem" of the Jews in Europe was to kill them. He had already rounded up most of the Jews and sent them to live in concentration camps. Then he turned the concentration camps into death camps. By 1945, six million Jews had been put to death by Hitler in places such as Dachau and Auschwitz. Hitler's "final solution" became known as the Holocaust.

Chapter 29 Test

Sequencing: 3, 5, 1, 4, 6, 2

7. Vichy France
8. Dwight Eisenhower
9. Battle of the Bulge
10. Albert Einstein
11. Harry Truman
12. Hiroshima

13. After German soldiers invaded Denmark, they began what was called a "Lightning War," or Blitzkrieg, by sweeping down the coast of Europe, through the Netherlands and Belgium, and invading France.

14. Winston Churchill called the German U-boats the "worst evil" faced by the British soldiers.

15. On D-Day, Allied troops landed on the beaches of Normandy in France and began to advance into France.

16. When President Roosevelt ordered government scientists to begin figuring out how to build an atomic bomb, it was known by the code name "the Manhattan Project."

17. After World War II was finally over, the United Nations was formed.

18. The most pressing job of the United Nations was to try to convince the nations of the world to stop developing atomic weapons and to disarm the weapons they already had.

19. Even today, people argue about President Truman's decision to drop the atomic bomb. Some people say that the killing of so many Japanese men, women, and children who were not soldiers, and were not involved in the fighting, can never be justified. Along with the thousands who died when the bombs exploded, hundreds of thousands more died later on because the nuclear fallout caused them to develop cancer and other diseases. Others say that by dropping the bomb, the United States prevented many more years of war, in which many more people would have died—because the Japanese had no intention of ever surrendering.

Chapter 30 Test

Sequencing: 1, 3, 5, 2, 6, 4

7. Indian National Congress
8. Pakistan
9. Kashmir
10. Zionism
11. United Nations
12. Arabs

13. Muslims disliked the Hindu belief in many different gods because Muslims believe in one god, Allah.

14. When India gained independence, fifteen million Indians left their homes because Muslims were scared to live in a country ruled by Hindus, and Hindus were scared to live in a country ruled by Muslims.

15. Nathuram Vinayak Godse assassinated Gandhi because he was so angry that Gandhi had allowed India to be partitioned.

16. The Holocaust caused Jews and non-Jews to become more interested in the idea of a Jewish homeland.

17. Egypt, Lebanon, Iraq, Jordan, and Syria all invaded Israel on the very day that independence was declared.

18. To everyone's amazement, the Israeli army managed to win the war.

19. Creating the nation of Israel caused such a problem because Arabs had been living in the land of Palestine for the last thousand years. The Arabs considered Palestine their homeland. Jews also considered it their homeland, even though they had not lived there since the year AD 70 when the Romans drove them out. Their sacred scripture told them that God had chosen that land for the Jewish people and that one day they would return to it. Jews everywhere rejoiced when the United Nations voted to give part of Palestine back to the Jews, but the Arabs in Palestine did not want to give up their land. The Arabs who lived in the nearby countries of Syria, Lebanon, and Egypt were also angry because they did not want to see their fellow Arabs lose their homes.

Chapter 31 Test

Sequencing: 3, 2, 5, 1, 4, 6

7. United Arab Republic   8. Suez Crisis   9. Dwight Eisenhower

10. Secretary of State   11. France   12. Berlin

13. When President Eisenhower refused to give Nasser a loan, Nasser became so angry that he closed the Suez Canal.

14. Israeli troops invaded Egypt because Egypt had banned Israel from using the Suez Canal, and Israel needed to show that other Arab states couldn't bully them.

15. The Eisenhower Doctrine was a law that said that U.S. soldiers could go and fight on the side of any Middle Eastern country that asked the U.S. for help against an attacking army.

16. Countries in Europe needed help after World War II because businesses and banks were out of money and many buildings had been bombed and needed to be repaired or rebuilt.

17. The Marshall Plan was a plan to bring stability and peace to Europe in which the U.S. would give twenty billion dollars to the countries of Europe so that they could rebuild.

18. Joseph Stalin refused to accept help from the United States because he thought that if he took money from the U.S., America might one day ask him for a favor, and he was sure he didn't want to do whatever America might ask.

19. After World War II, Germany was divided in half. Great Britain, France, and the U.S. got to re-organize the western half. They helped set up a new German democracy, and used Marshall Plan money to rebuild Germany's roads and buildings. The Soviet Union turned the eastern half of Germany into a communist country. They decreed that the other Allies could have nothing to do with East Germany. For several years, people could travel back and forth between East Germany and West Germany, but many people began to stay in West Germany because life there was easier and freer than life under the communist government. When the East German government realized that it was losing too many scientists, university professors, doctors, and lawyers to the west, they closed the border and would not allow anyone else to leave.

Chapter 32 Test

Sequencing: 4, 1, 5, 3, 2, 6

7. African National Congress   8. Afrikaners   9. apartheid

10. Red Army   11. Taiwan   12. the People's Republic of China

13. The National Party thought Afrikaners should control the government of South Africa.

14. Black South Africans used nonviolent resistance to protest the Unjust Laws. They refused to carry their identification cards, and when police arrested them, they didn't resist.

15. The South African government threw ANC members into jail, and anyone suspected of joining the ANC was followed, spied on, and reported to the authorities.

16. Millions of Chinese joined the Chinese Communist Party because they had lost their jobs during World War II and had no hope of making enough money to buy food and clothing.

17. The Kuomintang army had run out of money and hadn't paid its soldiers for months. Many Kuomintang soldiers had been earning money for food by selling their guns to the communist soldiers.

18. Mao and the communists executed over a million people who supported the Kuomintang, and twenty million people were sent to concentration camps and prisons, some of them simply because they were rich or considered "Westernized."

19. One of the acts passed by the National Party was the Population Registration Act, which divided the population into four groups: white, African, colored, and Asian. Under this act, only whites had full privileges. The Immorality Act said that whites could not marry anyone from the other three groups. The Group Areas Act made many areas in cities off-limits to non-whites. The Separate Amenities Act said that non-whites had to use separate buses, taxis, movie theatres, restaurants, and hotels from whites. The Bantu Education Act said that Christian missionaries could no longer educate black children. Instead, blacks would be taught in government schools that only got one-tenth of the money spent on white schools. Yet the textbooks in these black schools explained how good the separation of the races was for South Africa.

Chapter 33 Test

Sequencing: 5, 2, 3, 6, 1, 4

7. Viet Minh   8. Hanoi   9. Cochin China

10. 38th Parallel   11. General MacArthur   12. Harry S. Truman

13. Chiang Kai-shek didn't trust Ho Chi Minh because Minh was a member of the Communist Party, so he threw Minh in jail for eighteen months.

14. Ho Chi Minh allowed the French to put military bases in Vietnam because the French promised to leave the Democratic Republic alone to rule itself as a sovereign country.

15. At the end of the French Indochina War, Vietnam was divided into two parts. The north would be a communist country with Ho Chi Minh as president, and the south would be a separate country and hold its own elections.

16. After World War II, the Soviet Union set up a communist government in the north part of Korea called the People's Republic of North Korea.

17. The Chinese got involved in the Korean War because they were worried about being invaded when British and American soldiers pushed the communist forces so far north that they almost reached the Chinese border.

18. The truce that ended the Korean War said that the north would remain a communist country known as the People's Republic of Korea, and the south would remain the Republic of Korea with an elected president, and the 38th parallel would remain the border.

19. After World War II, Korea had been ruled by Japan for so long that there was no Korean government left that could step up and run the country when the Japanese left. Korean officials had to learn how to govern their own land. There were also hundreds of thousands of Japanese who had to be moved back to Japan. The United States and the Soviet Union decided to divide up the responsibility for slowly giving Korea back its independence. Although this division was supposed to be temporary, neither the U.S. nor the Soviet Union was willing to move out because both countries distrusted the other.

Chapter 34 Test

Sequencing: 2, 5, 1, 4, 6, 3

7. junta   8. Mussolini   9. Evita

10. MNC or Mouvement National Congolais   11. Katanga   12. Zaire

13. Italians and Germans who had settled in Argentina during the 1800s wanted their country to join the Axis powers, but other Argentinians wanted to join the Allies.

14. Juan Perón became popular with the working poor by introducing laws that made sure that working people were paid a fair wage and had money to live on when they were too old to work.

15. Perón made sure that he kept his power by using Fascists methods. Anyone who objected too loudly to his reforms and laws was likely to mysteriously disappear.

16. Before Europeans had settled in Africa, the area of the Congo had been divided into many small territories, each the home of a different tribe. Many Africans thought that the Congo should go back to being many small, independent states, each governed by its native tribe.

17. Mobutu gained power in the Congo during the civil war when military officers seized control of the country. Four years later, Mobutu gave himself the title "president" without holding any elections.

18. Mobutu kept his power in the Congo by arresting those who disagreed with him, accusing his enemies of treason, and sending out spies to find out whether anyone was criticizing him.

19. King Leopold II of Belgium mistreated the people of the Congo in many ways. He forced them to pay high taxes. To earn enough money to meet the king's demands, Africans had to work long hours making rubber or go on dangerous elephant hunts so that they could sell the elephants' ivory tusks. Leopold allowed slave traders to raid the Congo, taking Africans to sell in Europe as slaves. Every village in the Congo had to send four people every year to work as slaves for Leopold. He even made a notorious slave trader the governor of part of the Congo.

Chapter 35 Test

Sequencing: 6, 1, 3, 5, 2, 4

7. Sputnik   8. NASA or the National Aeronautics and Space Administration

9. Neil Armstrong   10. Florida   11. John F. Kennedy   12. the Bay of Pigs

13. When the Soviet Union launched its first satellite, the United States was worried that the Soviets might use their rockets to carry powerful weapons over to the U.S.

14. When the Soviets sent the first man into space, the Americans were determined to work even harder on their space program.

15. The first astronauts on the moon left an American flag to show that Americans had won the space race and a plaque that said, "We came in peace for all mankind" to show that their accomplishment was greater than a simple political victory.

16. When Fidel Castro gained control over the Cuban government, he began to turn Cuba into a communist country.

17. After Fidel Castro gained power, thousands of Cubans left Cuba because they had lost their businesses, they were afraid of arrest, and they could no longer say freely what they thought.

18. The U.S. invasion of Cuba was unsuccessful because word leaked out ahead of time, so that when the invasion force arrived, Castro's soldiers were waiting.

19. After the Bay of Pigs, the Soviet Union sent weapons to Cuba. When American spy planes, flying over Cuba, took pictures of nuclear missiles and jet bombers, Americans were terrified. President Kennedy sent U.S. ships to surround Cuba and keep any more weapons from coming in. He then warned the Soviet Union that if a nuclear weapon were dropped on the U.S., America would attack the Soviet Union. The Soviet Union prepared its own troops and announced that it would fight back. For thirteen days, the United States and the Soviet Union were at a stand-off over the missiles. Finally, the Soviet Union offered to take its nuclear missiles back, as long as the United States would promise not to invade Cuba. The United States agreed, and the Cuban Missile Crisis was over.

Chapter 36 Test

Sequencing: 6, 4, 1, 5, 3, 2

7. Dallas, Texas   8. Camelot   9. Lee Harvey Oswald

10. Jim Crow laws   11. Martin Luther King, Jr.   12. Civil Rights

13. President Kennedy was popular because he was handsome and well-spoken. He graduated from Harvard. He was married to a beautiful, charming wife, Jacqueline Bouvier Kennedy. He was a war hero who had served in the Navy during World War II. He had written two famous books and won the Pulitzer Prize.

14. After President Kennedy was shot, his vice-president, Lyndon Johnson, became the new president.

15. Lee Harvey Oswald was shot by Jack Ruby while millions of people watched on live television.

16. In the case, Brown v. Board of Education, the Supreme Court ruled that racially segregated schools violated the Constitution.

17. After Rosa Parks was arrested, leaders of the civil rights movement organized a boycott of the Montgomery buses, and they took the bus company to court and accused it of violating the Constitution.

18. The president had to send federal troops to escort nine black students to school because the governor of Arkansas would not obey the Supreme Court order to desegregate schools, and he sent National Guard troops to prevent the black students from entering the school.

19. Before President Kennedy was assassinated, America had been prosperous, excited about the future, and filled with energy. Every man had a good job, people built houses more than ever before, and life seemed to be good. The problems in America lay below the surface, but after President Kennedy was shot, the problems—the Cold War, poverty among immigrants, segregation in the South—seemed to rise to the surface. Life in America seemed a little less glittering and a little less wonderful. Americans were forced to face up to the troubles in their own country.

Chapter 37 Test

Sequencing: 6, 1, 3, 5, 2, 4

7. Viet Cong   8. Richard Nixon   9. Saigon

10. Jimmy Carter   11. Camp David Accords   12. Nobel Peace Prize

13. A draft is when a country needs more soldiers than those who volunteer, so young men are forced to join whether they want to or not.

14. When American soldiers left Vietnam, the communist army resumed its attacks, captured Saigon, and took over the South Vietnamese government.

15. When American soldiers returned home from Vietnam, they were not welcomed as heroes. They were likely to be jeered at, or criticized in public by those who had opposed the war.

16. At the end of the Six-Day War, Israel took these territories away from the defeated countries: the Gaza Strip, the Sinai Peninsula, the West Bank of the Jordan River, and the Golan Heights.

17. President Nixon decided to send weapons to Israel during the Yom Kippur War because the Soviet Union sent weapons to Egypt and Syria.

18. Because the United States had helped Israel, the five Arab countries that made up OPEC refused to sell oil to the U.S. after the Yom Kippur War.

19. Vietnam was split into two countries. The north was a communist country, but the south was not communist. The American government was afraid that North Vietnam would invade the south and take it over. If that happened, the whole country would be communist. And if one south Asian country became communist, all the others might follow like a "row of dominoes." In 1959, fighting began between the South Vietnamese government and the Viet Cong (communist rebels). When China and the Soviet Union sent guns, ammunition, and supplies to the Viet Cong, President Johnson ordered U.S. Marines to go into South Vietnam.

Chapter 38 Test

Sequencing: 4, 2, 3, 5, 1, 6

7. KGB   8. defectors   9. Mujaheddin

10. Munich, Germany   11. Israel   12. Palestine Liberation Organization

13. People wanted to leave the Soviet Union because life under communism was hard, and it was difficult for them to buy the things they needed.

14. When the Soviets invaded, the Czechs were so unprepared for the invasion that no one had any weapons.

15. Afghanistan was not an easy country to conquer because the Mujaheddin knew how to stage guerilla warfare, attacking from the rough wild mountains of their country and then disappearing again.

16. The original goal of the PLO was to form a new homeland for the Palestinian Arabs who had been forced to leave their homes in Palestine when their land was claimed by Israel.

17. When a terrorist organization claims responsibility for its attacks, it calls international newspapers and explains who carried out the attack, and what they want.

18. When the IRA began to reject terrorism, some members split off and formed the PIRA because they thought that terrorism was the only way to ever get Northern Ireland back for the Irish Republic.

19. Terrorists fight by attacking civilians. They carry out random, violent acts against people who aren't involved in governments or armies. They set out to get what they want, not by defeating an enemy army, but by creating so much terror among the people of a country that the people force their government to do what the terrorists want. They want the rest of the world to know what they are doing because they hope other countries will recognize their demands and pressure their enemies into meeting their demands. So they claim responsibility for their attacks by contacting international newspapers and television stations. They hope that if they can get their demands in newspapers and on televisions, people all over the world will see, understand, and sympathize.

Chapter 39 Test

Sequencing: 3, 4, 1, 5, 6, 2

7. the United States   8. Bangladesh   9. the Punjab

10. Mohammad Reza Shah Pahlavi   11. ayatollah   12. theocracy

13. East Pakistan wanted to be free from West Pakistan because the government offices and the army headquarters were in West Pakistan, and East Pakistan was becoming poorer and poorer while West Pakistan prospered.

14. The Sikhs decided to use the Golden Temple in Amritsar as their headquarters because it was a religious shrine and therefore off limits to Indian police.

15. At the Union Carbide Corporation's factory in Bhopal, twenty-seven tons of methyl isocyanate poison leaked from a tank and killed thousands of people and made thousands more horribly sick.

16. When Iran seized control of the oil fields in Iran, the British refused to buy any more oil from Iran. At the same time other countries started pumping more oil than ever, so there was too much oil in the Middle East, and too few buyers in the rest of the world.

17. During the Iranian Revolution, millions of people began rioting in the streets and forced the shah to flee the country.

18. Iran and Iraq fought an eight year war because they both wanted to control a river known as the Shatt Al-Arab.

19. During the White Revolution in Iran, the shah worked on making Iran more modern and more Western. He gave women in Iran the right to vote. He tried to improve schools and give more Iranians the chance to get an education. He tried to make religion less powerful in Iran. He changed Iran's calendar, so that it no longer followed the traditional Muslim calendar, and he told religious newspapers and magazines to stop criticizing the government.

Chapter 40 Test

Sequencing: 4, 3, 1, 6, 5, 2

7. Arco, Idaho   8. Eisenhower   9. Pennsylvania

10. the Gipper   11. Mikhail Gorbachev

12. Scientists and government officials were excited about nuclear power because they thought it might be an inexpensive source of electricity, and countries wouldn't have to rely quite so much on gasoline and oil.

13. The accident at Three Mile Island frightened the people who lived nearby because the plant operators hadn't been able to figure out how to stop the radiation from escaping, and it had taken scientists so long to measure the radiation that escaped.

14. The accident at Chernobyl spread radioactive particles all over the Russian countryside and into parts of Europe. Six hundred thousand people were exposed to dangerous levels of radioactivity, and animals became sick and gave birth to deformed offspring.

15. Perestroika allowed ordinary people to have more control of Russian businesses, and even own their own businesses, instead of the government owning everything.

16. Under glasnost, people in the Soviet Union were given greater freedom of speech, and it was no longer a crime for newspapers to publish criticism of the Soviet government.

17. The INF Treaty declared that both the United States and the Soviet Union would get rid of weapons that were short range (weapons that could travel only three hundred to thirty-four hundred miles).

18. President Reagan believed that the key to ending the Cold War lay in the way that both countries would deal with their weapons. Neither country wanted to get rid of all their weapons because they were afraid the other country would not keep its promise to do the same. So Reagan decided to invent new, bigger, and more powerful weapons. He believed that, if the Soviet Union knew America had weapons stronger than anything belonging to the Soviets, the Soviets would be too afraid to attack. This strategy was called "Peace Through Strength." America could ensure peace by being stronger than any other country.

Chapter 41 Test

Sequencing: 4, 2, 6, 3, 1, 5

7. the Soviet Union   8. Red Guard   9. Deng Xiaoping

10. television   11. Boris Yeltsin   12. Russia

13. When the Chinese government forced farmers to combine their farms into collectives, harvests plummeted, grain grew scarce, and a famine swept over China that killed thirty million people.

14. The Cultural Revolution was the time between 1966 and 1976 when every part of Chinese culture had to praise Mao and Mao's policies.

15. Deng Xiaoping returned some of the farms to their owners and told peasants that if they raised extra food, they could sell it and make a profit. He also let the factories give up making bad steel.

16. Life in East Germany under communism was hard. There were few jobs, not enough food, and East Germans couldn't leave their country and go west.

17. After the gates to the Berlin Wall were finally opened, the Germans began to tear it down with shovels, tools, and iron bars.

18. After the communist conspirators gave up, Gorbachev met with Boris Yeltsin, and he banned all Communist Party meetings, and ordered every Communist Party office in the country locked up.

19. In April of 1989, thousands of students joined together in Tiananmen Square and demanded that the leadership of China change. They wanted to be given a chance to take part in China's government, and they wanted to elect their own leaders. The students refused to leave unless China granted them democracy, but the Communist Party wasn't willing to give up power. The Communist Party sent the army to warn the crowd to disperse, but the students refused. More people began to join them. On June 4, the army attacked the unarmed protestors. Over a thousand people were killed. All over the world, people protested the violence, but when it was over, the Communist Party still controlled China.

Chapter 42 Test

Sequencing: 1, 6, 3, 4, 2, 5

7. the UN   8. Baghdad   9. First Persian Gulf

10. Desmond Tutu   11. F. W. deKlerk   12. Nelson Mandela

13. When Saddam Hussein invaded Kuwait, many nations worried that if Hussein stayed in Kuwait, he would not only control the oil that Western nations needed, but that he might next invade Saudi Arabia and control even more oil.

14. The United States, Saudi Arabia, Afghanistan, Great Britain, and Egypt were among the twenty-eight countries that helped free Kuwait from Iraqi control.

15. As they retreated, Iraqi soldiers set the oil wells of Kuwait on fire.

16. When the Tutsi invaded Rwanda and began to drive out the Hutus, at least a million Hutus had to flee to Zaire where they had to live in camps. With so many people in the camps, food and water were scare, and many died from hunger, thirst, and disease.

17. The UN put an embargo on weapons, so that no one could sell guns or ammunition to South Africa.

18. The United States and other nations refused to lend money to South Africa or to buy South African goods.

19. Saddam Hussein invaded Kuwait for several reasons. Iraq had borrowed money from several countries, including Kuwait, during the Iran-Iraq War. Kuwait insisted that Iraq pay its war debts, but Hussein couldn't afford to. Hussein also claimed the Kuwait was taking oil from a patch of land on the Iraq-Kuwait border. He said that half of that oil should belong to Iraq. He also said that Kuwait was producing more oil than OPEC allowed, and that this was making the price of oil too low, which was like taking money away from the other countries that produced oil. Finally, Hussein said that Kuwait was actually part of Iraq anyway, and he was just reclaiming what belonged to him.